A Letter to a Brokenhearted Ghetto

By Julius Edwards

P. O. Box 2535

Florissant, MO 63033

Copyright ©2012 by Julius Edwards

All Rights reserved. No part of this book may be reproduced or transmitted in any forms by any means, electronic, mechanical, photocopy, recording or otherwise, without the consent of the Publisher, except as provided by USA copyright law.

All scriptures are taken from the King James Version of the Holy Bible.

The events in the book are actual and factual.

Edited by: Kendra Koger

Cover Designed by Sheldon Mitchell of Majaluk

Manufactured in the United States of America

Library of Congress Control Number: 2012941977

ISBN: 9780983486077

For information regarding discounts for bulk purchases, please contact Prioritybooks Publications at 1-314-306-2972 or rosbeav03@yahoo.com. You can contact the author at: *king_julius4@yahoo.com*

Table of Contents

Acknowledgements	i
Dedication	iii
Introduction	vii
Chapter 1- Communities	1
Chapter 2 - LIFE	17
Chapter 3 – Success and Failure	23
Chapter 4 - That Bitch and That Nigga	29
Chapter 5 - African and American	35
Chapter 6 - In our Community there is much pain	45
Chapter 7 - Predestined before our birth	55
Chapter 8 – The power to Rise	65
Chapter 9 - The Ghetto	69
Chapter 10 – The Enemy's Conversation	73
Chapter 11 - Our Broken Hearts	77
Chapter 12 – GOD	81
Chapter 13- Lost and Found	85
Chapter 14 – ATTITUDE	95

Chapter 15- THOSE POINTS 99

Chapter 16 – CONCLUSION 109

Acknowledgements

I would like to thank my pastor. Pastor James E. Buchanan has been supportive. I thank him for his spiritual guidance. I want to thank Lonnie R. Lynn Jr. for his positive outlook on my life. I would like to thank my Family and Friends for their endless love and support.

Dedication

This book is dedicated to our communities and the people who live in them. We can become better and we will.

A Letter to a Brokenhearted Ghetto

Introduction

In order for us as poor and oppressed people to become part of a society that is meaningful, the system under which we now exist has to be radically changed. . . It means facing a system that does not lend its self to our needs and devising means by which we can change that system. – Ella Baker

I have searched for answers on why and how our people came from Africa, to slavery, to a point of cultural defeat; and why our ancestors' paths and messages makes a huge difference. I wonder what purpose do drugs, violence, ignorance and poverty serves in our communities. Only to find out it serves no purpose but to break our families, take our people's lives, leaving our children hopeless and to leave us in pain.

The system has taken our minds off who we are, where we were headed and for us to lose focus on our goals and on our culture's victory. They knew once we were free, wholeheartedly, spiritually, mentally, physically, and financially, it was a wrap. They know the only hope of the enemy ever being able to subjugate this country is by residing in principal cities, such as: Washington D. C, Philadelphia, Detroit, St. Louis, Chicago, New York City, Los Angeles, Houston, New Orleans and other great cities. So they cause chaos in our cities to make us think and feel like we have nothing and make the ghetto seems worthless. Therefore, we destroy what we have, but in reality we live in the best parts of this country and don't realize it. Jeremiah 29: 7 states: "And seek the peace of the city whither I have caused you to be carried away captives, and pray unto the LORD for it: for in the peace thereof shall ye have peace." Instead of allowing ourselves to feel entrapped in our neighborhoods, we need to regain our agency in it. Peace comes in the freedom of knowing that we and our neighborhoods are strong.

We have to ask ourselves why they never wanted us to be free and to have nothing. We've got to ask ourselves why was Martin Luther King Jr. , Malcolm X, Huey Newton, Tupac and so many others were assassinated. It wasn't their physical bodies they wanted to assassinate, it was the message they carried, and who they represented is what they wanted to assassinate. Let's question why white people concealed our true history. They had to find a way to keep us under their control, so they came up with this ingenious plan and system to imprison our minds as well as our children's minds. Where the mind goes the man follows. So they gave us guns, drugs, welfare and projects and made laws that target us. America has always been at war for independence, either for the nation, a race or for an individual.

What I have come to understand is it's a war for the hearts, minds, souls and freedom of mankind. The devil and government are against us. Either we play a part of our independence or fall into captivity from the devil and the system. They don't want us to know the power we hold within, and the opportunities that present themselves to those of us that are willing to stand for something. Most of us think our problems are money, but money is not always the problem; common sense, not taking care of our priorities and allowing others to define us is the problem. I want us to understand we have opportunities other African American generations wish they could have had and we waste them on selfish attitudes/actions.

The ghetto is a place that really tests our faith. At times we ask ourselves, why try? Why have faith? It seems as though the ghetto is where all the odds are against the people; a place where it seems poverty, ignorance, pain, stress and the suffering will never come to an end. This is where brothers are divided by a dollar, and sisters divided by penis; where families are broken. This is a place where right seems wrong and wrong seems right; a place where insanity passes as sanity and where the average person is living on the edge. The feeling of being confused, overwhelmed or trapped by the struggles and situations is the norm for its inhabitants. It's always tempting for us to try to make those feelings and situations go away by taking the quickest and easiest action possible, but what we actually need to do is slow down and think. It's the only thing that will give us clarity to make the best choices; looking carefully at the situations, and examining all sides of it, both positive and negative.

America's system knows where we are in our lives because they think they know the mindset of ghetto people. Many white people think we all think the same as well as look the same anyway. They know the life they have created for us. It's difficult in the ghetto because there is no unity, respect, love, understanding and very few pursuits taken, as well as no organization nor discipline. We make it much harder than it should be. In the ghetto where we see and feel each other's pain and brokenness, due to the street mentality and the thug/five star image we act afraid to lend our support for fear that others may see us as weak. Instead of running from their pain people instead need to start embracing it. In the ghetto we all just about walk the same path, but our beliefs, steps, attitudes, minds, hearts, spirits and lives take us on different pursuits.

After our grandparents' and parents' generations get in older age it's up to our generation to carry on the legacy that was instilled in them. What are we going to carry on to, when some of us are getting locked up, killing each other, and just not caring? We're a generation that can't afford to be wasted or lost. We can conquer hate and poverty once we put down the guns and raise our voices. Let it be known, we are here and we're not going anywhere. The future depends on us, the youth. The older generation passed us the torch. We will have to carry it on in life and the message to the next generation. If you are ready, we can change the world.

Nas, the rapper said: *"We can break the cycle, let nobody lie to you. Then maybe put our sons and our daughters in private school, because there's a mission we have to finish before we leave. This generation is destined to do historic deeds."*

It's true that if we heed to the Bible and remember to be examples: *"Let no man despise thy youth; but be thou an example of the believers, in word, in conversation, in charity, in spirit, in faith, in purity"*. -1 Timothy 4: 12

Chapter 1- Communities

"When you control a man's thinking you do not have to worry about his actions." -Carter G. Woodson

Our communities are our homes, our lives and families. They shape us. However, we need to shape our communities for the better, with more common sense, love and accepting each other. We all live in the same environment with the same problems. We think we would be better off somewhere else. Truth be told, we can make it better for ourselves, others and those who follow us and look up to us right in the communities where we live. We are so quick to say "I love my city; this is my block," but look at the things we do to our communities. We need to make our communities safer and comfortable, not just for ourselves but for others as well.

Most folks in the ghetto want to make it out the ghetto instead of making a life for themselves and their families in these communities. Too many of us are so busy in the streets that we don't take time to realize anything. Moving out of the ghetto might seem daunting for those who can't even afford to eat on a daily basis. It shouldn't be moving out the ghetto that satisfies us, it should be moving the ghetto and ourselves out of the darkness. Look at how many lives were lost and families affected by our negative mindset. In America, a ghetto person has a choice of four paths: God's way, penitentiary, education or the grave yard.

We are the answers to the problems that each of us desperately needs. Our problems come because all we see are our needs and wants, thinking it's only about us when it's not! Once we take an eye off ourselves, we'll see the needs of our hurting communities and the needs of the world as a whole. Our communities are broken because we are in a cultural battle, but our selfishness and ignorance calls it to be an unnecessary individual battle. Our communities are ripped apart because we are lost in our lives and minds, we are lost in the battle of a dollar in success.

Going solo, we can only accomplish so much; but as a unit, we can help others and ourselves improve our living conditions, productivity and accomplish more.

"If we think we have ours and don't owe any time or money or effort to help those left behind, then we are a part of the problem rather than the solution to the fraying social fabric that threatens all Americans/People." Marian Wright Edelman

We need to quit being selfish with our love and support and spread it among the hated and haters. We have all this unreasonable hate built inside us, either because of he/she say, a dollar and sometimes no reason at all. We need to add some hope to our society.

We are chasing a dollar in the wrong places. We don't see the wealth because our minds and eyes are stuck on a dollar and what others have achieved. We are confusing a dollar with success. A dollar keeps us unfocused and keeps us blind to success. Success is what we are chasing a dollar for in the streets. See, we want the riches and the nice things and think by pulling licks and selling drugs we would be able to achieve those things. Proverbs 28: 20 states: "A faithful man shall abound with blessings: but he that maketh haste to be rich shall not be innocent."

We can achieve those things, but not by the street's way. A dollar brings about anxiety, divorces, divided family members, broken friendships, and sleepless nights. People are driven to crime, drugs, suicide and ruin lives over a dollar. A dollar keeps us on a hunt day in and day out, trying to find any way possible to make a quick buck. We must not become slaves to money. We must understand that money is essential to life under man's government. We are life and eternal souls under God's kingdom, and we must understand our ability to have great health, wealth and abundance through the power of God. A dollar leads astray with no leadership or guidance. That American dollar we want so bad comes with a price. Every dollar is counted and watched, it will never be ours. It will always travel from hand to hand.

Our dreams lead to self-belief, which leads us to believe in a higher power, which leads us to authentic and worldly success. But understand that worldly success doesn't come with us after death.

"Every great dream begins with a dreamer. Always remember, you have within you the strength, the patience, and the passion to reach for the stars to change the world." -Harriet Tubman

We are in a battle with the system of America and the devil who seek to destroy us. John 10: 10 alerts us that "The thief cometh not but to steal, kill, and to destroy…" So how can we war on each other? We rip our communities apart; yes, us, by violence, false hate, selfishness, poverty, lack of knowledge and misunderstandings. Joshua 7:13 tells us: *"Up, sanctify the people and say, Sanctify yourselves against tomorrow: for thus saith the Lord God of Israel. There is an accursed thing in the midst of thee, O Israel: thou canst not stand before thine enemies, until ye take away the accursed thing from among you."* The same way how Israel was in the midst of redemption, they couldn't achieve it without removing the things that caused conflict within their community.

Our society is at the same threshold. We will never be able to redeem ourselves unless we remove the things that cause dissension between us. Our communities are broken because we won't spread the things we truly have, which are ourselves, our love and our support for each other to reach and excel to new levels in our communities and personal lives.

With each other support we can go beyond the sky. It will take us places a dollar can't. If we knew the Word of God like we know raps and song lyrics we would have power and have direction. We won't spread our love and support because we feel as if we'll be looked at as weak/soft, or won't be accepted in a hated community, or the world. Proverb 29:23 read: "*A man's pride shall bring him low: but honour shall uphold the humble in spirit.*"

Truth be told, the ghetto is the only place we are accepted, because we all just about grew up together, and know each other; we're a family. The people of the U. S. A are always trying to deny us our rights, our ghettoes, and our existence; not only us but our own race of people as one. We help the U. S. A by showing hate among each other. Most folks in the ghetto only get records from killing, selling, robbing or petty crimes. That could be prevented! We need to learn to manage our own lives and listen.

We deny our own presence and make ourselves invisible to life by falling into the trap they have set for us. Although we know it's a trap it seems as if we don't even care and still fall victim to a corrupt system. Then once we get caught up in the nonsense we want to blame everyone else for the poor decisions we have made, after we have been told repeatedly where we could end up.

True enough, it's not our fault we were born into this madness. Psalms 51:5-7 reads: "*Behold, I was shapen in iniquity; and in sin did my mother conceive me. Behold, thou desirest truth in the inward parts: and in the hidden [part] thou shalt make me to know wisdom. Purge me with hyssop, and I shall be clean: wash me, and I shall be whiter than snow.*"

This shows us that though we are born into our situations, we can always have a way out if we ask for it. It will be our fault if we don't make the best out of life while we have time. How do we turn this madness into happiness? Easy, by not setting ourselves or our people up for failure. The people in these types of communities have already been set up for failure true enough so it's up to us people in the communities to turn it into a success together. We, people in the ghetto communities, are so focused on what we don't have that we don't realize what we do have (power is in the votes). Who can we vote for, when we are afraid and don't know the system?

"The power of the ballot we need in sheer defense, else what shall save us from a second slavery? To be a poor man is hard, but to be a poor race in a land of dollars is the very bottom of hardships."
-W. E. B Du Bois

These are our own voices, our communities, our own people, our own way of fun and life, our own money, homes, schools, churches and our united faith. That's all we need and each other and we can move mountains together. We may not have a rich bank account, but once we become rich minded and spirited then money will be no problem.

"And unto the angel of the church in Smyrna write; These things saith the first and last which was dead is now alive;I know thy works, tribulations, and poverty (but thou art rich) and the blasphemy of those who which say they are Jews, and are not, are of the synagogue of Satan." -Revelation 2: 8-9.

Please stop making poor decisions that hurt you and your family and our communities. It's not about a dollar, it's about living a happy life, comfortable and abundantly. The American government is all about a dollar. We are not from America; we're just a part of America. The system of America is funny because they get a pat on the back for corruption and for making dirty money. When we make dirty money they want to throw us beneath the jail.

America wouldn't have made it this far without us, but now they wish they could destroy us all, and one by one they do so with our help. We have seen how crazy and foolish the devil and the U. S. A system would love for our cities/people to be torn apart. We cannot allow them and the stupid stuff to divide us from our loved ones, families and friends. We can't allow them to have their way, while we suffer from hurt and poverty. Let's see how BLESSED our communities can be now that we are releasing the curse we have carried for so many years. With the power of GOD and ourselves we can do this. Once we bless and pray for each other GOD can bless us individuality. The problem with so many of us is that we are in the habit of looking for blessings to be material supplies, when our first blessings must be spiritual, psychological and then physical. Prosperity can't flow into our life while our hearts and minds are filled with doubt, fears, or destitute thoughts and self-convictions. Our lives move in the direction of our thoughts, beliefs and our actions.

"There is no Negro problem. The problem is whether the American people have loyalty enough, honor enough, patriotism enough, to live up to their own constitution..." -Frederick Douglass

God can't bless us with a "forget the world" type attitude. We curse ourselves by cursing others; we bless ourselves by blessings others. In order to save ourselves we must reach a hand to save one another and put the selfishness behind us. Our communities are the only thing we have in the U.S.A. If we destroy our cities then we have nothing and nowhere to go. I understand that you want to live like the white folks, but understand the white folks moved out the cities because we moved in.

We've got to quit trying to live like them and understand how God wants us to live. Could it be like Joseph? He was sold into slavery by his own family and accused for false crimes and became a great ruler of Egypt, which was the same nation that put him in prison. Nelson Mandela served 27 years in prison just for seeking freedom in his own country from people who wanted to rule Africa and became a mighty man once he was freed. Could that be the destiny of the African American culture; a land full of kings and queens, or a land full of depressed, desperate and lonely people?

We are destroying our communities and then want to run to the white communities hoping to be safe when they put us at this point. They gave us what we wanted from them, which was our freedom, so why are we still running behind them? "Where justice is denied, where poverty is enforced, where ignorance prevails, and where any one class is made to feel that society is an organized conspiracy to oppress, rob and degrade them, neither persons nor property will be safe." -Frederick Douglass

At once a point in time all we had was hard work on plantations. We had to do what we were told to do. In so many ways we make our communities out of plantations because we enslave ourselves with our thinking and action.

Tupac Shakur quoted in the song Ghetto Gospel, "And peace to this young warrior without the sound of guns, I don't trip and let it fade me, from outta the frying pan, we jump into another form of slavery." When I read this I think about the emancipation which was passed on September 22nd, 1862, slaves still weren't free. They were actually freed January 1st, 1863. Some slaves fled the south and some stayed. Even though the emancipation was in effect, hundreds of thousands of African-Americans still remained in slavery. From 1863 the Negros migrated across America. The Civil War was from 1861 to 1865. It is still America's greatest war to this day. More than half a million Americans' lives were lost just for us to have freedom or to be kept captive.

America has been at war with Afghanistan for nearly a decade and spent billions of dollars on that one war. After a decade at war with Afghanistan they still haven't conquered the numbers of lives lost in the civil war or any other wars America had participated in; that shows the hate the system has for us. The Afghanistan war was nation vs. nation; the civil war was one nation divided into two to keep one race hostage. After spending billions and billions of dollars on wars and incarceration they still haven't helped the Katrina victims or the poor. Does it speak for itself that they don't care, or that they never will? I understand America is a free country and we must spend billions of dollars on militarily to remain free, but when the government is against its citizens there's a problem at the top of the food chain, because we're at the bottom.

The Brown v. the Board of Education was a case to keep us from integrating in white schools, which was in 1954. The boycott issues happen in 1955. The Civil Rights Movement in the 1950s and 60s were to grant us our rights and freedom by the Constitution and not by man. In the 1900's we had race riots repeatedly; black vs. white. The riots were war on us; they couldn't defeat us so they turned the later generations on each other or a great many of us.

"The history of a movement, the history of a nation, the history of a race is the guide-post of that movement's destiny, that nation's destiny, that race's destiny." -Marcus Garvey

The rights of the Constitution, the Declaration of Independence and also the Bill of Rights are totally different from the rights man wants us to have. They still want to control us and give us what they want us to have so they can take it back whenever they feel they need to. When we don't understand the country we are from, or the country we live in, we will always be lost.

Understand how you were born where you are and how your family got into that situation. Martin Luther King Jr., stated in his "I have a Dream" speech in 1962, "A hundred years later the Negro is still not free!" Remember, that was 1962 and it's been about 50 years since then. There was a plan for our lives and for the generations to come if we don't break the curse now. Before they could put their plans into action they had to assassinate Martin Luther

King Jr. , Malcolm X and Medger Evers. All of them got assassinated in the same time period. It seemed as though there was a goal to erase our history and make it seem like we were nothing but slaves, but we are so much more than just slaves. Why did they take our history and only give us the European versions?

"Those who have no record of what their forebears have accomplished lose the inspiration which comes from the teaching of biography and history." -Carter G. Woodson

Merriam Webster on-line dictionary defines the word civil means- citizens, of or relating to citizens *b*: of or relating to the state or its citizenry <*civil* strife>. The word civil war means a war between opposing groups of citizens of the same country based on the same source. The word faction means- a group within an organization, united against others in the organization. What was the reason for the Civil War?

The Civil War was neither to save nor free slaves. The war was because the north was seceding from the south and thousands of blacks flocked to enlist in the army but were rejected. Blacks knew that the Civil War was an opportunity to end slavery; they knew slavery was tied to the union's victory or defeat. Neither the south nor north expected the war to last 4 years. Abraham Lincoln may or may not have had plans to free the slaves; he mainly wanted to save the union. As the war continued he changed his policies about slavery. He had to free the slaves if he wanted victory. After the emancipation we had nothing and nowhere to go, so we migrated across America to the inner cities.

The end of the 1800s and the beginning of the 1900s was chaos for blacks and the whites. Whites didn't want blacks in their neighborhoods, schools, restaurants; they wanted nothing to do with us. They wanted to be segregated from us. From the moment of the emancipation they wished they could find a way to destroy us all or ship us back to Africa. The Civil War was a white man's war but a black man's fight for freedom.

From 1960 we started to lose our way and the pursuit we were on as a culture of people. 1970-80s, guns and drugs hit our communities super hard and we lost our way. They gave us projects and welfare and we got satisfied with nothing, then we turned on each other. They took our minds off what was important and now it seems we don't care about anything other than some Jordan's, Nikes, clothes and rims; not even our living conditions. The slave system was created to make money, break families and sell them off and to keep the Negro in line and under control. The only escape was for the Negro to run away and leave for good. Just like today, we want to escape and run away from the ghetto to a safer place and think we would have a better life.

"There is no escape - man drags man down, or man lifts man up."
-Booker T. Washington

How can we not make changes in our personal lives to become better people and develop? This is our time; let's not let it pass by again. We are not going to make it with the hatred in our minds. We need to fix the ghetto, not ruin it or run from it. The problems will always remain until fixed. The jail system does the same thing the slave system did, make money and break families. The only difference is the people are free to live but because he/she is a slave in their minds, they can't think for themselves like they should be doing. 148 years later we enslave ourselves; going in and out of jail for petty crimes, killing each other and breaking our own families, leaving our children to be hopeless.

If this is what so many people give their allegiance and lives for, we could have stayed on the plantations. At times I wondered why did Martin Luther King Jr. , Malcolm X and so many others stood up for us? I wonder why Abraham Lincoln signed the Emancipation only for us to turn our backs on what it took for us to get here. Can't you see the system is created to break, dehumanize and dissocialize us to keep us from life, liberty and the pursuit of happiness? As long as there is stupidity and chaos among us we won't notice anything. Until we take off the blinders we'll be blind with seeing eyes.

We do stupid things to divide ourselves from our families and once we go to jail or get killed our children are lost in the system, only to be lost in life. We don't have anything in the U. S. A but ourselves and our race of people. Once we lose the false hate that we have among each other then we can see a better future. The one thing the U. S. A does not want is for us to be a free race spiritually, mentally, physically, financially and for our families to be broken.

"At the bottom of education, at the bottom of politics, even at the bottom of religion, there must be for our race's economic independence." -Booker T. Washington

Some White people want to destroy you as a person and us as a culture of people. Keep in mind that they want our families broken. They would be fearful of the fact that we have unity among our communities. Unity is power! Power, truth, wealth and independence are what they are trying to hold back from us, but they can't. However, we do a great job at keeping ourselves defeated and ignorant. We are powerful individuals. We can't be enemies with each other and our unknown family members and expect to have peace.

It is essential for us to learn to take it easy and exercise our minds so we can understand what we're trying to avoid and destroy. We have come too far on our life and our culture's journey to turn back or give up now. We should better our communities and ourselves so we can help better a nation/world. We have to break

America's spell immediately. America is designed against us and they blame us for their screw ups! I don't think we truly understand who we are and the opportunities we have.

It took us over four hundred years to get to this point. Now that we have made some progress we act fearful of moving forward in the middle of a crisis. The U. S. A hasn't given us nothing in four hundred years, what makes you think they are going to give us something now? We must create our own way of life and future. We'd rather live in the past than create a future with the present. Our own stupidity is what traps us. Our own ignorance is what keeps us from using our intelligence; our dependency is what stops us from being independent. Our fears of what ifs, is what keeps us from progressing. The situation we were placed in, it's not fair, but we have to find the truth somewhere in this man-made lie.

The whole government is all for power, cash and using us American citizens as guinea pigs. We've got to look through their game. Their system denies us and tries to deny the kingdom of God. Impossible. God's kingdom is within the human heart and to be on earth forever. Daniel 2: 44 tells us: "And in the days of these kings shall the God of heaven set up a kingdom, which shall never be destroyed: and the kingdom shall not be left to other people, it shall break to pieces and consume all these kingdoms and it shall stand forever." Most of the politicians are just looking to gain power and cash without accepting their responsibilities as the leaders. Letting the American people suffer so they can hold a title and gain power/wealth through deception. The American people have the power when we stand together and realize it.

GOD gave us power, love, gifts and talents and a sound mind to promote our life, but we use it for the opposite. He gave us everything we need to succeed, but we make up excuses. It's like trying to teach a bird how to fly, they have a natural ability to fly, you can love it, feed it, embrace it and one day you pray it will do what it is born to do; leave the nest and fly high, not by force but by choice.

It's like us in a way, we have a natural ability to live and grow, a mind to comprehend, a heart to love, a life to live, and a mouth to speak and smile, but we refuse to use these things for our best.

I don't know what makes people think that life is in the streets, in violence, or in hate. Life ordinarily starts in the heart and the mind of a human. The power and love is in the heart of the human. The intelligence and the ability to comprehend are in the mind. Remove the hate and stupidity and allow love and intelligence to take its place. In the ghetto we are lost in the titles we carry, we try our best to keep our reputations.

We never want to lose our rep because we don't want to be classified as a so called "lame." What is a lame? Is it a person with no material values? Is it a person with no understanding of him/herself? Is it a person who follows the followers? Why must we know the truth in our hearts, but due to popular opinions we fail to follow our own hearts? In our minds and hearts we want to lose the reputations and move forward with life, but why can't we? The ghetto won't let us, or is it us that we don't want to do better? Why? The ghetto is afraid to move forward. Understand the ghetto is not the streets that connects; it's the people in the communities. It's the way we live, the way we think, the way we eat, the way we treat each other, it's our mindset. In order to move the ghetto forward we must change and be better persons ourselves.

We've got to start thinking better, using more common sense, losing the tough guy/girl attitude. It's necessary we lose the false hate, selfishness, and the all-about-the-dollar mind frame. We have to gain more respect, courage, dignity and more trust in God. Having more faith in each other, and somewhat depend and support each other is important; the hardest part is going to be trusting each other. It's never easy to trust a soul, especially when people can't trust their own families. Respect and unity is something we must have in order to move forward. Somehow, some way, we have to complete an incomplete task. It's going to take the entire ghetto to rebuild each other and our communities.

We are so stuck in the moment that we don't prepare or think for the future. When the moment prepares us for the future, if we don't pay attention now then the future will pass us by and we won't even notice until we reach elderly age and wonder where life went. We are a brother and sisterhood of imperfect lives searching for perfection. The ghetto has a way of making us believe we can't grow when we really can, making us believe life has no meaning when it really does. We war on each other to survive, and hunt for a dollar when the pursuit is really to attain wholeness. We must understand that we are living and we mean more to the ghetto than the ghetto mean to us.

In order for us to grow and survive, we must grow into strong mature men and women, and not grown boys and girls. We have to cultivate the ghetto into better communities as we grow. The ghetto has life, meaning, and growth, and it's all found within us. We are the future of our ancestors, ourselves, our children and our culture. The only way we are going to get there is together.

"The choice is not between violence and nonviolence, but between nonviolence and nonexistence." - Martin Luther King Jr.

Our communities need to be indestructible and we can get there if we stick together as a whole. Once we lose the selfish mind frame, only then will we be able to progress forward. They work as a whole against us, so we need to work as a whole for each other. Without our freedom we have nothing. We need each other more than we think; to strengthen and support each other and to fix our culture crisis. We, African Americans, are our own empire and economic system. We can have our own Fortune 500 companies from state to state, city to city. Just like we destroy our cities and each other we can build each other up. It's been over four hundred years and we still have nothing, until we support each other and build our own empire we will continue to have nothing.

    We need to have some cultural identity. The time is now, it's time for all of us to reunite and make a difference in our communities and the world as a whole. Why can't we be a race that is not divided because of others' preconceived notions? We need to create our own jobs, build our own building and hire our own people. This is how you create opportunities and grow strong sons and daughter who in turn will create our future. We could have strong communities, progressive businesses and a solid economic system? Who's looking out for our best long term living abilities? We can redefine the ghetto. I don't know if we're just going to settle for their accommodations or if we're going to move into our own nationalism. Jeremiah 3: 21-22 reminds us: "A cry is heard on a barren heights, the weeping and pleading of the people of Israel, because they have perverted their ways and have forgotten the Lord their God. 'Return faithless people; I will cure you of backsliding.'"Yes, we will come to You, for are the Lord our God.'"

If a race has no history, if it has no worthwhile tradition, it becomes a negligible factor in the thought of the world, and it stands in danger of being exterminated. -Carter G. Woodson

Chapter 2 - LIFE

"I hope you can understand it, life can change your directions, even when you ain't planned it. All you can do is handle it, worst thing you can do is panic. Use it to your advantage, avoid insanity manage to conquer every obstacle, make impossible possible. Even when winning's illogical, losing's still far from optional." -T. I.

Life is spontaneous. As we grow we will come to understand that there is so much that we won't understand, and the only things we really know is that things don't go as planned. We will eventually face death. Life is so deep, but we want to stay on the surface of our fragile flesh, and when our hearts break from beneath our physical bodies, we wonder why and how. It's because we were always meant to live from our minds and hearts. But we're afraid because we live life based on flesh; so life breaks our hearts to force us inside to see the treasures, but we still don't go inside, we run. Romans 7: 24-25: "O wretched man that I am! Who shall deliver me from the body of this death? I thank God through Jesus Christ our Lord. So then with the mind I myself serve the law of God; but with flesh the law of sin."

The ghetto life hurts on so many different levels, and no one seems to care, not even the ghetto people; and we're the ones in the most pain. Do you think the government cares about us or our families? They hated us from the beginning until now. The hate that the system has for us to go almost as deep as the love God has for us.

What's crazy is we accept the hate from them, but won't accept the love from God. We can't have hate among each other and expect to excel. We want to be so strong and hold everything in, as if we have it all together; but we're broken behind the flesh. We want to let it all lose but think we will look weak because we shed some tears and released the frustration that holds us hostage. It's okay to cry. It's better to let it out than hold it in.

What happens to our tomorrow if we don't take our stand today? After centuries of trying their best to destroy us, they haven't succeeded. Now we are at a point where we are destroying ourselves and our race of people. We are continuously going deeper into poverty and crime by choice. We always want to point fingers and blame other folks when we're the problem.

We need to start blaming ourselves and taking responsibilities for the decisions and children we have made. We are making our children's lives more difficult than the life we once lived. We are leaving our children without love and guidance. We are leaving our children in the darkness of life because we refuse to shine our lights and step up. . We must accept the blame and go from there.

Either we take our stand now or fall with the ability to stand. The way I see it is we can only stand because we have been down face first for too long. We must stand for the greater good. We either create success or live in poverty. They think they have learned our strengths and weaknesses, and designed a system just for us. The thing they don't know is our ambition, the love and power of our hearts, the strength of our souls, the power of our spirit with the power of GOD behind us can't nothing stop us, but doubt.

It's time we face the reality of these situations and take our stand as the men and women that we're meant to be. We've got to push forward and overcome the obstacles of the ghetto life. We have to create a future for ourselves, our children and their children. Once we put down the guns and stop the useless violence only then will we be able to see the importance of life and not so much of the garbage. The only way our ghettoes or hoods are going to be the way we want to live is if we do it for ourselves.

We know the things our communities need and the challenges

we face every day. As we can see they don't know what our needs are, if they had a choice we would be slaves. Remember, it's up to us to overcome. Open your minds and eyes, people, to see the bullcrap and understand it. We are in the need of change and the only change there is going to be is the change we make. The power is in us! We must free ourselves from the bondage of anger, excuses, guilt, fear and self-limitations.

We must take our stand or sit and continue to complain about something we have the power to change. We are at war with each other and forgetting about the war we have been fighting since day one in America. I don't think this generation truly understands who we are and what we stand for and how we got where we are. We are the offspring of slaves, the children of GOD and we stand for His glory. We need to take some time to ourselves and spend some time with GOD to realize who we are as a person and to understand our purposes here on Earth.

We have so much to offer this world and our lives. As long as we are divided, selfish and fearful then we stand for nothing, not even ourselves; and can only offer extra despair & hate. I wish we could heal our wounds, renew our minds and mend our brokenness and rise from self-defeat. Although we are at war with the U. S. A. , we are losing because are we at war with each other during the battle. The U. S. A has turned us against each other to make it easier for them to defeat us as one. Attacking each other is not going to solve our problems.

It makes the problems worse for us and easier for them. Think about it for a second, after we have attacked each other, we realize the stupid decisions we have made to have no outcome. Now the system is on our backs trying to sentence us to death or life behind bars over some stupidity; leaving our children to the system. We lose our life and freedom over petty reasons and leave our children hopeless. The only way we will be able to rise and conquer is by stop defeating each other over nothing.

Julius Edwards

All we have to do is use our common sense and open our minds and hearts to life itself. We need to stop making our personal life more complicated than it already is. We need to stop trying to live so easy and lazy, and accept our responsibilities and pursue our path towards wholeness. It's time we go get what's ours and not what belongs to others. We must stop accepting what they give us to shut us up. What they give us is nothing compared to our needs and wants. Welfare and projects are nothing. Too many people live in the ghetto, many are unemployed and most of the females are on welfare or underemployed and receiving something from the government to make ends meet while many of the children have one parent or the father is absent. If they cut off welfare and Section 8 how will our families eat and where will our families stay? Too many are uneducated and thus they sit around and gang bang, shoot, and kill innocent children over careless reasons.

We claim territory and fight to the death over land that was there before us, and going to be there after us. I understand you want to stand in defense of our hoods, but must I remind you we came from a slave plantation, we need to stand in defense of each other. It's not just our ghettoes that suffer; it's our people's lives around the Nation/World. If we can overcome our situation of slavery we can do poverty the same way and spread hope across the world. We changed the world forever when we elected a black man, we can change the world again for the better. You see, they need as many of us to be eliminated as possible; the ghetto is on its way to a 3rd world living rite before our eyes.

In some places it's already there. If they can destroy us in our childhood, teens, youth or prime, they have succeeded and they use us to do so. We are too focusing on garbage that doesn't matter. Why must our cities be a war zone? Why must our cities be beautiful but we live like we stay in a trash dump? Why must the ghetto trick our newborns into believing life has no meaning? Why can't our children play outside, why must the ghetto rob our children of their childhood? Why must we live so low and narrow minded? Why must our memories be like nightmares? Why must our children need parole officers and social workers for guidance? Why must we wait on a hand out? Why do we do wrong when we really want to do what's right? Romans 7: 19 – "For the good that I would do, I do not: but the evil that I would not, I do."

Why are we afraid of change? Why won't we give life a chance? Why are we self-defeating ourselves? There is so much to do and so much to be done. We all came from God. Man was created by God and birthed by woman. (Genesis 2: 7 – And the Lord God formed man of dust of the ground, and breathing into his nostrils the breath of life; and man became a living soul). In Genesis 3: 19 God stated "from dust we were created and dust we will return," and if we just think about that we know that's true. How? What is a cemetery? A place where the dead is returned to the dust. Don't let the last message you hear be ash to ash, dust to dust. Don't wait 'til Thanksgiving to give thanks. Don't wait 'til Christmas to give gifts. Don't wait 'til Valentine's to share love. Every day is an opportunity for valuable learning to enjoy life and have a grateful heart. In life we have a choice to live and be free with the love of God or to be kept in man's trap of money and lies.

As we go through life we will understand we will have times of despair, hope, faith and love, even on our path toward wholeness. The object of life is development, growth, in mind, heart, soul and body, being renewed by Christ.

Chapter 3 – Success and Failure

"Prosperity is not just having things. It is the consciousness that attracts the things. Prosperity is a way of living and thinking, and not just having money or things. Poverty is a way of living and thinking, and not just a lack of money or things." -Natasha Chavis

Everything we need for our personal success is already inside us. Our true nature is like our own personal gold, waiting to be mined. Success comes from successful seeds. Success doesn't come from stupidity or standing on the block day in and day out or sitting around smoking and drinking all day. Success comes from successful imagination, visions and dreams with the willpower to bring them into reality. Our imaginations need a creative outlet for us to do our best work and the outlet is our reality. Confidence, self-control, self-discipline, preparation, patience and accepting personal responsibility prepares a person for success or failure. A part of success is planning ahead. Success or failure can lasts a life time.

Failure can always be overcome. The Bible tells us *"He that covereth his sins shall not prosper: but whoso confesseth and forsaken [them] shall have mercy."* (Proverbs 28: 13) We can only succeed after failure only when we acknowledge our mistakes and learn from them.

Success can bring joy and pain. Money is not everything; it's the way we go about making money and what we do with it that makes the difference. Don't wait until it's too late to pursue life. We aim for the smallest things though we want so much bigger and better. We can have better and bigger if we go for what's ours?

What's ours? Our dreams, goals, intelligence, ideas and our faith. The love and promises of God are ours. We have so much given to us to be accepting nothing. Remember, success lies in the imagination of the mind and in the power of the heart. Back in the day they wanted us to be stupid. But why? I came to the point because they know knowledge is power. With knowledge we can succeed at anything. Education is success, so put your minds to use.

Open your hearts and minds. They wanted us to have a lost life, they wanted us cursed. We must think for our ghettoes and not let our ghettoes decide our paths. The streets don't have a mind, it has a trap, so we must use our minds. They always wanted us to fall right before their eyes, but not just fall, fall into their trap and apart from our race. Therefore we won't be able to stand together with our faith and unity together.

They created this system so that they will be able to guide our life without us even knowing or notice. To give us the sense of thinking we guide our own life. Once we make that ONE stupid decision that they are praying and patiently waiting for. Then we are in their court rooms or jail cells; whatever it takes for them to make an example out of us.

They always wanted us under their control, that's why they never wanted us to be a free race. They didn't divide us, we divided ourselves. Now that we are free to live life for ourselves, and our ancestors who made these days possible, we spend it hating, killing and also destroying each other's' lives and our children's lives over street fame. We do unnecessary things to one another to please a system that doesn't care about any of us. The only things they give us are liquor stores, drugs, guns and label us a number to acknowledge us. They could care less about us or our ghettoes. They are praying we kill each other so they can reclaim their cities/country.

The quicker we realize that the faster we can move forward. The truth is visible, but invisible to those who accept the lies as if they do care. We can point fingers at them all day, but that gets us nowhere. We can't accept the life they planned for us. We must mount up our wings and pursue the life GOD planned for us. We can't allow them to determine our destiny as if they are our God. We must get off this path of destruction.

They know once we get on the right path it's a guaranteed success. Our success and power is something they fear as a race of people. At the end of the day it's our life we create or destroy. Just remember, poor decisions and a poor mind leads to a poor way of living. We must think twice before we make a decision that will ruin our entire life and future in less than 48 hours. We can't allow others to select our path to success or failure; at the end of the day it's personal decisions.

We must chase our lives, goals, and dreams at all costs. We need to take time to strategize and make a list of things we would like to accomplish for ourselves and our communities, and make it happen. A person with no plan plans to FAIL! Think about the big picture. We've got to start thinking smarter, not just for ourselves but for our families and our communities. We can't settle for what we don't want. Life is meant to be lived and not substituted with fear, pain, or excuses, nothing but exercising faith.

We need to address the fact that our ghettoes are our homes. We have to find a way to turn the ghetto into communities. The only way we are going to turn the ghetto into communities is by attacking the devil and the system that is attacking us all. Not by walking into that trap they set for us, but by finding a way to fix it. The thing is the ghetto people feel that life is in the ghetto, but the system and TV makes us believe our lives would be better off elsewhere.

We think our lives would be better if we lived in a white community, or somewhere else other than our homes. You know how people say the grass is always greener on the other side? Well I found out that's not always true. The only thing we have to do as a community and people is water and take good care of our own lawns and it will be greener than the other side. The soil is the same, it's just how people treat their garden of life.

The American system would love to keep our lives broken. They would love to keep us believing that a dollar is the answer to everything. Remember, the more money we have the more problems we attain. We are the solution to our culture problems and GOD is our personal answer. It doesn't take a rocket scientist to recognize the trap we are in. We don't even try to get out; we fall deeper into the hole. They don't even want us to have a peace of mind. African Americans have accomplished so much in the U. S. A so we need to finish the pursuit.

If we get on our stuff here in America we would be a world movement. If Martin Luther King Jr, was the last message we heard about in the 60s, what's the message now, and what was he trying to tell us? Why have we given up on everything our people slaved for? Because we are too busy trying our best to destroy our ghettoes and each other's' lives, and thinking life is all about sex, drugs, clothes, money and parties. We could be using that energy and time on building our future. It's not that we can't accomplish anything, but we don't even try to achieve our personal greatness.

We are too busy trying to achieve material values which have no meaning, but we think it means everything. We think material things defined us but it doesn't. It shows what we have and not who we are. The world judges us by our skin color, not by what we have or our character and we act as if it's okay. We can't allow people to label us as nonhuman because of our skin color.

Our struggle doesn't come 100% from the system. Our struggle comes from us only wanting a simple dollar and wanting to pull licks on each other and making our personal life a competition. We only try to make it through the day, but what about preparing for the future? The system of the U. S. A is almost created like the prison system. Where they can keep the power and wealth to themselves and keep us in the cave of our lives, until we choose to step out. Therefore they keep us in poverty and make us have disorder in our communities, so they can keep us in order with that system.

They always wanted us to be lost, either in the streets or in the system. The system is created to try to break us, for us to fail ourselves, our minds, spirits, souls, heart and personal greatness.

> *"And like His [God] promise is true Only our faith can undo,*
> *My only bleedin' hope is for the folk who can't cope,*
> *With such an endurin' pain that it keeps 'em in the pouring rain,*
> *Who's to blame for shootin' caine into your own vein..."*
> *-Lisa "Left Eye" Lopez, "Waterfalls"*

It's easy to recognize it only when the truth is sought after. So many people in the ghetto don't seek the truth; we just want to play it safe by making a dollar. Trying not to take any risk on going beyond the ghetto's mind frame. The only risks we take are penitentiary risks. We don't want to better ourselves nor our communities because if we did we would.

We just want to blow up and show up. We just want money and think everything is going to be okay, but no. If we don't grow up there's no point in blowing up, because it will all be gone before we can decide what's next. We can have all the money in the world, but if we don't know how to manage it, or what to do with it, it will be gone as fast as it came. Money is cool to have, but it doesn't make the world go around. God allows the world to turn until the Apocalypse comes to completion. If money rules the world, what rules the universe?

> *"What has made me successful is the ability to surrender my plans, dreams and goals to a power that's greater than other people and myself..." -Oprah Winfrey*

Money buys us nice things, pay our bills and bring fake, deceiving people into our lives. Money is cotton our people slaved for, and never had enough to live. We all are trying to discover our next steps in life and think money is going to get us there, but no, our pursuit is. The decisions we make today determine our next moves.

The ghetto is at a standstill, but the world is constantly turning and changes while we are changing for the worse. We need to mold the ghetto as the world turns, and quit being passed by. We can't allow people to look down upon us and we can't look down on ourselves. Money is meant to be spent, success is meant to be enjoyed, and life is meant to be lived. People say it's a white man's world and money is everything. I say it's only a white man's world because we refuse to take our place in this world and money is only everything in man's economy. There's nothing wrong with having wealth, we just can't serve riches. If it was something wrong with wealth God wouldn't have promised to give us the power to have wealth. A successful person is wise and strong enough to build a foundation with the stones. Our life can be a journey to great prosperity, success and happiness, but only if we discover and use our personal gifts and qualities that were assigned to us at our birth. Only then will we achieve our full potential.

"Success is to be measured not so much by the position that one has reached in life, but by the obstacles which he has overcome while trying to succeed." -Booker T. Washington

Chapter 4 - That Bitch and That Nigga

Everybody in the ghetto wants to be the same person, same thing. Which are the wrong people and the wrong things? See, we all have a destiny and purpose to fulfill but some of us take short cuts and arrive later and some never arrive, but those who do arrive on time are those who pursue life. To be cool, some want to be drug dealers, a so-called gangster, or a nickel and dime hustler. They want to be at war with the neighborhood, people that grew up with each other.

Everybody wants to be classified as somebody they can't hold the title to, such as the bitch or that nigga; titles that have no meaning. Everybody in the ghetto is already on one page, but it's the wrong page. Everybody is competing to be a person who doesn't exist or who got this or that. That's not to say that we can't have one sharp mind, and move as a people, because we do that now. We've got to have one mind frame and move as a people to defeat the enemies who are defeating us all. Only if we can turn it around for the betterment of ourselves and the communities like it was before the drugs and crimes hit out communities, then we would be better off and can continue our freedom and rise from poverty.

We all want to get to the next point in life, but we take the wrong steps, and start off on the wrong path, trying to advance to the next level. Not really listening nor thinking it through, or probably not caring. All we know is we want to be "that bitch" or "that nigga" and make a little extra cash, and want people to notice us. But the questions still remain. Who is that bitch or that nigga? What makes her that bitch? What makes him that nigga?

"1 out of 3 black men in their 20's is out on bail, probation, court supervision, community service or parole or behind bars. . ."
-Bruce Dixon

Who is That Nigga?

    s "that nigga" the drug dealer who spent 80% of his life in and out of jail, and spent his drug money on paying off the system? Is "that nigga" the doctor who spent 80% of his life in school discovering his life passion and became successful? Is "that nigga" the so called gangster who can name every gun, but can't name his father? Is "that nigga" the preacher who tries to tell us about God, but we think he's crazy? Is "that nigga" the guy who's just a baby daddy and won't step up to accept his responsibilities as a man? Is "that nigga" the dude with a couple hundred dollars and think he rules the world? Is "that nigga" the president who is from the ghetto and spent his life following his heart on an im(possible) mission? Is "that nigga" the guy who carries a gun just to impress his peers? Is "that nigga" the guy who starts his own company? Is it the nigga with a few women and thinks he's Don Juan, or the nigga who's ten years older or more than the chick he has sex with only to play with her mind. Is it the nigga who turn his back on his people for a few dollars?

    Is it the nigga who put his hands on a female just to feel big and bad? It doesn't make us "that nigga" because we are so-called pimps and players but can't find a wife and won't take care of our children. Fellas, why can't we take the pain we issue out? It takes courage to step up, but most of us can't see past our own penises, to realize what's real. Fellas, we need to use our power, faith and influence to overcome what we think we can't do.

Who is That Bitch?

    Who is "that bitch" and what makes her "that bitch? " Is it the chick with four kids and four different baby daddies, and on welfare? Is it the chick that starts her own business? Is it the chick who works for hers? Is it the chick who fucks the average nigga just to feel accepted? Is it the chick who won't let a guy touch her unless he has more than just sex to offer her? Is "that bitch" the chick that's searching for a father and a friend, but looking in the wrong places?

Is it the chick who sleeps with her best friend's man? Is it the chick who finds her own husband? Is "that bitch" the chick who wants a baby just because she thinks the nigga is going to be hers? Is it the chick that lowers her standards just to please a guy who don't even want her? Is it the chick that turns her back on her people because she thinks she got a nigga who's going to be there forever? Is it the bitch that puts a nigga before she puts her kids? Is it the chick that goes clubbing every day and leave her kids stranded? Ladies, quit trying to keep a nigga that's not trying to be kept. Ladies, let go of your insincerities. Females, you need to have more respect for yourself. Anybody can be "that bitch" or "that nigga." Is "that bitch" or "that nigga" the person who dropped out of school just because they think the streets have something to offer them. You are worth more than you know.

Who is "that bitch" or "that nigga?" Is it the person who ruins their life just to feel as if they are somebody in the streets? Is it the person who builds their life from nothing, or the person who turn their back on their people? I need answers I'm confused on who's "that bitch" or "that nigga." I need to know the qualifications this person must have. The thing is our minds are in the wrong places. We no longer think for the betterment of ourselves, even though we believe we think we do.

Maybe because we can buy, eat, have sex and go wherever the wind blows? We are misplaced in this lost society, and we think because we can do anything and live, like standing on the corner and sell drugs and go clubbing, that we are free. That's a way of deceiving the enemy. We can't turn our backs on our families and friends; those are people we don't get twice in life. The system uses military tactics on us to deceive our minds; they look at us like we're the enemies. They got us thinking the opposite of the truth and got us focusing on comparing ourselves to others.

The goal is to keep our minds off what they have on their agenda. We are stressed from lies and material lust. We are distracted from the importance of life and no longer focus on the message of Christ. We don't even try to comprehend the message Martin Luther King Jr, and Malcolm X and so many others that left us. They warned us, but we act like we don't care about anything but what we want. We have been given this delusion of what life is through TV, music, internet and video games and allowed popular culture to deceive us to thinking and believing the way they want us to comprehend. We have allowed man to create our way of life, create a false society and give us a false identity.

We act as if it's okay. No, it's not. We are living in poverty and attacking each other over nothing, letting them get away with capital one murder. They are making us look stupid, while they are making billions and billions of dollars off us acting like some idiots, and we can't get a full course meal, find our way out of debt, or get a job.

Our ignorance feeds their families and ours are starving. As long as we sit around and be the system slaves then we get what we get. There's no way possible we can't take our fate in our own hands and rise. Like Ne-Yo said, "we're a movement by ourselves and a force when we're together."

"Cops give a damn about a negro? Pull the trigger, kill a nigga, he's a hero." -Tupac

A young man named Sean Bell was killed by excessive police force, but there are so many others is another reason why we need each other. They know we're a force together, that's why their aim was to divide us. We can rule the government, the government doesn't have to rule us, but they will if we don't say something or take our stand as citizens of America.

"The power is in the people and politics we address, always do your best, don't let the pressure make you panic, and when you get stranded, and things don't go the way you planned it, dreamin of riches, in a position of makin a difference." -Tupac Shakur

The power is in us, we can sit around and live miserably and continue to be their stools or take our stand. The U. S. Government, the system of people, for the people, and by the people, but what about us, the ghetto people who's being left out? Why are we being ignored and why are we ignoring ourselves? Knowledge is power and once we know the knowledge we have in our unconscious minds, then we will be able to make conscious decisions. We are so caught up in nothing, that we don't even notice the wool that's been pulled over our eyes.

We don't even know what's been going on in Washington DC, or the rest of the world; as if it doesn't affects us. They are trying to take the rights we don't even know we have, the rights so many fought for; the ones we don't use. We need to stop worrying about Tom, Dick and Harry and pay more attention to life and what's really going on, PLEASE! We can't tell what's next because we don't know what's going on now. We are so sure of where we're heading, but have no idea because we are forgetting where we came from.

We are from American slavery and we are still on the path of gaining our Civil Rights, but it was interrupted in the 1960s. After Martin Luther King, Malcolm X and Megar Edgar got assassinated it paralyzed our culture. Then the crime and drugs hit our communities and turned it into a war zone and we lost focus on what was important. Since the 1970s the incarceration and the death rates have sky rocketed and only going higher, because we refuse to pay attention and stand together. If the average guy in the ghetto isn't dead or in jail he's on his way there.

One of the reasons some people who lives in the ghetto can't get a job if they tried, is because they have a felony and think it's hopeless. That's how the conservatives try to take our freedom and life by affecting our conscious decisions and distracting us.

They don't want us having anything; you can't even work at a fast food place with a felony...

But God said that when we repent our sins, we become clean. *Isaiah 1: 16-20. 16Wash you, make you clean; put away the evil of your doings from before mine eyes; cease to do evil; 17 Learn to do well; seek judgment, relieve the oppressed, judge the fatherless, plead for the widow. 18 Come now, and let us reason together, saith the LORD: though your sins be as scarlet, they shall be as white as snow; though they be red like crimson, they shall be as wool. 19 If ye be willing and obedient, ye shall eat the good of the land: 20 But if ye refuse and rebel, ye shall be devoured with the sword: for the mouth of the LORD hath spoken [it].*

You can change but you have to pray and live according to the Bible and God will wash you as clean as snow. Never give up or feel put down. Put your trust in God, not man.

Chapter 5 - African and American

African is our identity and culture which we don't understand. We are too busy trying to understand the American wealth. We don't even understand America and how she came to be America and what she means. How can we live the way God intended us to when we don't know who we are and won't comprehend our purpose and keep forgetting where we came from? IT'S IMPOSSIBLE!!! Being a black person in America is not easy. Male or female, the hunt has been on before entering into America and we and our children are the prey.

We are confused in our minds. We don't want to listen to anybody who tries to educate our minds and give our hearts faith. We listen and trust those who take away from our minds and life. When someone tries to warn us about the path we're on, we have this type of attitude as if 'I don't wanna hear this garbage, you can't tell me what to do, I'm grown,' and we don't know the first thing about being grown, thinking we know everything.

"I freed a thousand slaves I could have freed a thousand more if only they knew they were slaves." -Harriet Tubman

We only want to protect our pockets, but what about our lives and our children's lives and freedom; we take it for granted. They use us to serve their purpose and to feed their economy. If we can't serve them, or they can't use us, then we are useless to the American politicians.

AFRICA

"Whereas our ancestors (not of choice) were the first successful cultivators of the wilds of America, we, their descendants, feel our-

selves entitled to participate in the blessings of her luxuriant soil."
-Richard Allen

Africa is a land which our ancestors where took from and brought to America, not by choice. Not for the benefit of their selves, or for us, but for the benefit of the people who brought us here; to be broken, sold, to pick cotton, to give free labor, to produce slave babies and to serve the whites. Our ancestors have always stuck together because of their unity and faith, united they had power and strength. Many of them knew they needed each other to survive in America.

We we're supposed to be slaves, but somehow we are a generation that has been set free from physical slavery (Thank God Almighty). Somehow, we enslave ourselves with our thinking and actions. We haven't bettered ourselves or our culture. Why? We are stuck with a narrow mind that won't allow us to travel outside our appearances or our so called "image." We only want folks to see us with the latest gear, brand new clothes/shoes and any car with rims and materials we think are of value.

On the other side we have deadbeat parents, staying from house to house, depending on other folks for a little change in our pockets. But as long as people see us with the latest fashion then life is all good, right? FALSE! Why are we so afraid to step out our comfort zone? Afraid the U. S. will see us as a misfit. Well, let me tell you a secret. We're all misfits in America. America is a nation of misfits seeking freedom, life, liberty and the pursuit of happiness. The system of America has ripped us away from our identity. They have broken our homes, taken our family members and stolen our lives. The government of the U. S. should be on trial for murder, kidnapping, lying, stealing from the Americans and also breaking their own laws.

America is more of a mental thing than physical today to make you think and believe the opposite. But both mental and physical work goes hand in hand. The American government has turned the people against one another to take focus off of them. In some African-American culture there are those who still lives in poverty and in slums across America, which could be turned into communities, only if we, the people, are willing to spread our love and support and add some intelligence to our minds. Open your eyes, and minds to life and the importance of our communities, ghettoes, slums and our people.

The word community is to describe a more unified set of people. The word ghetto has turned to describing something as stupid, or a set of inhuman people who don't know anything but how to be stupid. The word slum is to describe an area of living in super impoverished and a third world life. People notice them but show little care, if any care. Today, the American part of us African-Americans is destroying ourselves and our culture of people. One by one we are disappearing. Why?

Although we don't want to destroy each other, we feel as if that's the only way to get ahead. That's a false way of life. It's simpler than that. We just have to reach out to help build each other up and we'll find ourselves building our personal life.

"Rest in the Lord, and wait patiently for him: fret not thyself because of him who prospereth in his way, because of the man who bringeth wicked devices to pass." –Psalms 37: 7

We, Africans-Americans, today are continually forgetting the African part of our identities and only focus on the American wealth. It seems as if we don't know the difference, or don't care.

There's a huge difference between African and American. The African's land is the birth place of all mankind. The African land is rich, yet there are poor African-Americans who are poor. Why? The African part of us is the natural caring people who would lead a helping hand to our fellow brother or sister. The African part of us is the person we know is true, only on the inside, but can't find the courage to bring that person to reality. The African part of us is the people who would take care of our entire family, community and the whole world if we could. The African part of us is the loyal powerful warrior. The African land is spiritual land. "African" is our identity, it's so much more to us than just ignorance and material wants.

The American people took us from this identity and gave us one that does not fit our personality. We have adopted this non-existent character and were trying our hardest to bring him or her into existence. We can't move forward until we become authentic. I want us to understand that we are Africans in the land of America, which makes us African Americans; but first we're Africans! As the African race of people, we are all we have in America. Most American politics are against us African/ ghetto people. We, as African Americans, have gained a power that we are not fully aware that we have, we must pursue a better outcome for our people.

American

"The white, the Hispanic, the black, the Arab, the Jew, the woman, the Native American, the small farmer, the businessperson, the environmentalist, the peace activist, the young, the old, the lesbian, the gay and the disabled make up the American quilt."
-Jesse Jackson

America is a land of different ethnicities. It's not a land of one culture, it's a land of many different people from other countries. It is the land where every man is supposed to have undeniable freedom, liberty, rights, and equality. A land where we are free to bring ourselves to life with the opportunity to live abundantly! A land of pioneers, a land to prove the impossible, a land of dreams! A manmade creation with the help of the awesome Creator Himself! The American part of us is our dreams, the opportunity to bring our imagination to life, the all about a dollar and the material things type attitude.

The American part of us is the opposite of the African. The American part of us is the people who think we can do whatever to people and get away with it. The American part of us is not bad; it's just that we allow the government and the American prosperity to affect our conscious decisions. The greatest thing about America is that we, the people, rule. If we only knew that, not just us ghetto people, but all American people, together we could rule. The thing that can destroy America is the people being greedy, lazy and ignorant to the truth. Voting for the wrong people and doing nothing to promote life, liberty, the pursuit of happiness, and of course, God.

America is the UNITED States, but it's divided by selfishness, race, greed, dishonesty and ignorance. The Americans' selfishness & greedy way of life is what caused us to build walls around ourselves and not trust people. Once we restore our faith, unity, hope, love, charity and justice then we, the people, will be united. The reason we can't move forward, or why we feel trapped, is because we are living a life of self-consciousness and intimidation of others. Once we uncover our authentic selves we will be able to climb mountains and cross oceans that seemed impossible at once-a-point of time and live fearlessly.

First, we must get our minds sane, so we can build ourselves and our culture here in America and across the world. In order to change the world we must change ourselves, our thinking and our behavior. The only thing America gave us was a free green card; American politics want to destroy the African race. People across the world wish they could have the opportunities we have. America is an awesome land, but the love of money is what destroys us all. We neither can be like the boy, Calvin, in the movie "Like Mike," searching for a family, or the fools in the movie "The Lady Killer," getting great wealth but kills themselves, or the chicks in "B. A. P. S," going after opportunities but finding themselves living their dreams. America is not a white man's land. It's the land of the Almighty GOD. America is the modern day Garden of Eden, but the evil is in the people; being greedy, selfish, and judgmental.

We have to cast the demons out of our souls and off our land to become better people. America is a great country, full of blessings and ungrateful people who take our blessed land and prosperity for granted. Such as: water, food, shelter and opportunity. This is a land full of selfish people who only count their losses and never take time to give thanks for their blessings. America is the land of freedom, but it seems they only want free labor from us. What free labor means to them is free money and us doing nothing with our lives but wasting it in the streets or in jail.

The African American part of us is God's property. Once we wake up from the American dream and realize we're living the American nightmare, then we will be able to progress. America is a land where people can bring their dreams and ideas to reality. America is the freedom for which mankind search for. The only dreams that come true are those we bring into reality. A land of human rights, businesses, ideas, dreams, visions, goals, innovations, it's a land of science. Wake up from the nightmare and live the dreams God planted within your heart.

"Visions that can change the world trapped inside an ordinary kid which looks just like you, who's too afraid to dream out loud, And though your idea is simple, it won't make sense to everybody, You need courage now If you're gonna to persevere. Keep the dream alive don't let it die It's something deep inside that keeps inspiring you to try, don't stop And never give up on you."
–Yolanda Adams (Never Give Up)

We must realize what our dreams are and take the necessary

steps to bring them into fruition. Nobody ever said it would be easy; so we must keep God in our hearts, and don't give up before due season. The people who created the system of America over the last 100 years have placed us in uncomfortable zones, and in uncompromising situations. The American system has given us an identity and a lifestyle that we are not proud of, people we don't want to be, or people we don't know. We think we have to be those examples they want us to be in order to survive. We don't! We are made up of the two of the greatest countries mankind knows of, Africa, and America. When you think of Africa you should think of kings, queens, royalty, greatness, wealth, the beginning of mankind, a place of a timeless and complex history; not just the negative things. *"And hast made us unto our God kings and priests: and we shall reign on the earth."* Revelation 5: 10

We need to be the real us. The people God created us to be. God has a plan for our lives. He stated in Jeremiah 29: 11, "For I know the thoughts that I think toward you, saith the Lord, thoughts of peace, and not evil, to give you an expected end," so we need to get back on His team. We must kill the negativity and bring the real us to life. We are living in pain and hurt because we bring it on each other. We choose to live the way we live because we refuse to fight the battle that's trying its best to defeat us all. We'd rather fight with each other then take a stand on the foundation that's already been set for us.

We'd rather destroy our piece of communities, rather than rebuild ourselves and our neighborhoods. We'd rather be what the media want us to be, rather than be who we're meant to be; and live in hurt, rather than heal the silent pain. We act as if we can't overcome adversity and we help them divide us rather than stand strong together. We want to hide our pain and put on a strong attitude as if we have never been hurt, or not hurting. We show our weaknesses by not using our strength and power to rise from an undefeated battle.

We are a sad race of people because we'd rather be looked upon as a sad race. With the system against us and we being against ourselves, we will never excel to the next level. We want to play it safe by not growing within life, but life is passing us by right before our eyes. The reason we can't live the life we want to is because we are ignoring our personal life, self-expression and trying to be like everybody else. Trying so hard to live the life of the suburbs and live like others. The only difference between the ghetto people and the suburbs people is that the suburb people take care of themselves and their communities.

They use their common sense and work hard to provide for their families and stand together. Some ghetto people have a negative attitude and that attitude screws up all our lives. There's an absence of standing together and an abundance of only thinking about self. I understand you want to live like the people in the suburbs, and you can, right in the community where you live.

Our ghetto is us, our people, and our way of thinking and actions. We can move the entire ghetto population to the suburbs and in a short amount of time we've turned the suburbs into a ghetto because of our mentality and the savage behavior. We can move the entire suburbs of people in the ghetto and they will turn it into a community with jobs, houses and have success. We must change it ourselves, by changing ourselves; therefore, we can transform the ghettoes. Our ghettoes are in the best places of America, why do you think some white people want to reclaim the cities. Waiting for the people in control to change it, it will only get worse. It's crazy in the hood, but it's only crazy because we make it that way by doing nothing but destroying and feeling sorry for ourselves. They expect us to dwindle and live like nothing and nobodies.

We keep waiting for handouts and the only handout they're giving us is handcuffs. They brought us here in cuffs and they're taking us out in cuffs and body bags. If they were going to change it they would have never placed us in this situation in the first place.

The only things worth having is the things we work for, nothing comes free. There are great examples of people who live great without welfare or sections 8 in our cities; it's up to us to live the life we want.

We ghetto people have the ability to rise from poverty and pain only if we do it together. Hurricane Katrina is the perfect example of why our communities and race need to stick together, because it took the government nearly a week to go to their rescue. Now, if the average black community was doing as well as it needed to be, we would have been able to help ourselves. But because so many black communities are falling apart due to crime and lack of resources it feels like we are living like hurricane victims with no hurricanes, we're waiting on FEMA that will never show up.

It seems like most of the government could care less about us. Therefore, we need to focus on the assignments we have at hand. We need to quit all the unnecessary gossip and have more real conversations. We need to stop destroying each other and help build each other personally. We need to have more self-love, self-confidence, self-respect, self-worth, self-esteem, have more self-discipline, and be more self-reliant. We need to be more self-determined and more self-sufficient and quit always wanting to blame others for our failures and decisions.

We need to clean up our image and take care of our hygiene. We need to have more patience with life and quit trying to live so fast, we're already ahead of our time. We need to lose the insecurities; it's nothing but a lack of confidence, and learn to control our emotions. Beauty and handsomeness goes beyond the skin and body, it's inside out. With each of those above things we can move forward, and help each other on our way. Selfishness only makes us injurious to ourselves and isolated from life and others. The world was created for us to enjoy.

We need to change this played out scene, and change it to more of a concord scene. Most of us have children and we can't curse their lives. They didn't ask to be here, we chose life for them, and we just can't walk away from their innocence. It's our children's turn now to grow up; and what way of life are we teaching them? Although we sometimes act like we're nothing but grown kids we need to start making adult decisions. It's time we grow from our past. It's time we forgive ourselves and others; holding on to whatever past mistakes, losses, heartaches, only hold us back. Whether we realize it or not there's a reason behind everything we do or don't do.

Every choice we make or avoid we have a reason to. We must go forward, but we can't until we acknowledge what's holding us back. What's holding the ghetto back is the system with our help, the feeling of needing to escape the ghetto as if we are trying to run away from a plantation. We will never escape the ghetto because we are the ghetto. We, people, made the ghetto the way it is; the ghetto didn't make us hateful, evil or stupid, our actions made us that way. The only escape is to free the ghetto of the evil spirit that hunts our souls and quit living the man-made lie. Why won't we let go of what's holding us back?

Chapter 6 -
In our Community there is much pain

The average person is in some form of pain. A pain nobody cares about. Why must we be in the present of our lives, but be so distant? You know how guys join gangs and females run to prostitution? That's pain of not being accepted, or being molested, or a need to feel safe. Sometimes we join the gangs just to seem cool and to feel like we belong somewhere. Sometimes people prostitute just to find comfort or to make some money. Some children steal because they don't have parents or food at the house, that's pain of starvation. The pain and loneliness of being on our own and by ourselves can be unbearable for some. Why so much pain?

Some people just do stupid things because they have no guidance, or just because. There are some people who don't even care or refuse to help those in need. We walk around as if we are all good, but knowing deep inside we are hurting as if someone is ripping our hearts into pieces. The average person is in a pain that he/she can't even understand why or how. The pain of the ghetto is a pain by itself, and to top it off we have the pain of life.

The feeling of not being able to support our families, not being loved, being the outcast, being hated for the color of our flesh. The world will never understand the pains of the ghetto or the ghetto people. The entire ghetto is in a struggle. Do you think the government cares about our lives? Their behavior speaks for itself. It's going to take us all to embrace ourselves and our communities; we all share the same pain in one way are another. Open your eyes, minds and hearts, people. We can transform our ghettos and our personal lives at the same time. We can't escape the ghetto, it's our way of thinking, and we must change our thinking to escape the ghetto. We can't let our pain and struggles drive us insane. I can't understand why we don't want to free ourselves of the heartache.

We'd rather go time after time causing more confusion and anxiety to our lives and others' lives, not knowing that peace lies within.

The average person holds so much in. We act afraid to let loose and move on, not just physically, but mentally, emotionally and spiritually. We elide the most important things in life, which is ourselves, our ideas, gifts, love, families, success and our own lives. We'd rather chase the things that will always be, such as girls, guys and material values. We worry about the wrong things. We chase replaceable items. Life only happens once, it is not a game and there are no second chances. We can't sit around all day and play video games or be on the internet all day and expect time to wait on us. Life is meant to be pursued, happy, joyful, and successful, love, peaceful and understanding. We feel alone as if there is no one to trust, talk freely to, no one who understands our problems and pain.

The problem starts because we are not honest with ourselves. We know we shouldn't be in certain situations, but we still put ourselves in harm's way. We know there's more to life, but too afraid to step out of our comfort zones and don't want to go the extra miles. So we divide ourselves from life and only desire to get high or sell drug, chase hoes and niggas, and make money. Because we make a little money and can go shopping and partying and we think we are living to the fullest. But no! That's a false impression of life! We lie, steal, and hurt ourselves, putting ourselves in pain.

We cause others pain because we want someone to feel our pain, but don't know how to express or explain the brokenness of it. The pain we have we use to cut others deeper than our scars. The pain is mental, emotional, and spiritual; once we fix those we can live better. We think we could get by with pain on the inside while keeping a straight face on the outside, but we can't. Life is growth, learning, changing, developing, loving and overcoming, proving the impossible. We have a personal genesis and revelation; we need personal understanding. We can't cheat ourselves out of life. In between our personal Genesis and Revelations we write our stories as we go. What will your book of life read? The added pain and struggle is caused by us, the ghetto people, and we haven't realized it yet. Hip Hop is our cultural movement, it is to inform the people of the culture problems we still struggle with. Hip Hop is the voice that speaks to us as one people. She encourages, inspire and empower us to self-awareness and to community/world action.

Before then the system caused the pain to our ancestors by enslaving them, hanging them, burning their homes, letting the dogs loose on them, spraying them with fire hoses, hydrants, not letting them go here or there, controlling them; but I guess since it didn't happen to us, why should we care? We just forgot about what and who got us here.

We think so much has changed but nothing has changed; we just became ignorant to what's going on. I feel sorry for the later generations if we continue thinking it's all about money, weed, hoes, niggas, parties, and materials. I'm not saying you shouldn't have money, or nice things, or party hard. I'm saying just know there's more important things that must be done. They had to divide and break us because we were too strong together; and plus, we kept GOD first with our united faith. So they had to take our minds off what was important and GOD. We can't wait until it's too late to take our stand. WE MUST STAND TOGETHER AND BE STRONGER THAN BEFORE!

"We're going to do for blacks exactly what blacks did for the revolution. By which I mean: nothing." -Che Guevera

"I see no changes. All I see is racist faces...
We gotta make a change...
It's time for us as a people to start makin' some changes... -Tupac

We've got to create our own way of life for ourselves and our culture of people. They can't give us what we want because they don't know what we want or what our needs are. They only know so much about our way of life, but they threw us off track with life. That's why it's important for us to know where we are in life right now and our history.

We gotta quit depending on the system that enslaved us and depend more on God. We must lose the selfish attitude and greed and acknowledge the pain of the ghetto life, and the pain of each other's souls. We've got to start caring about something other than green dead presidents. I wish we would wake up from this selfish attitude that's keeping us from progressing to a better life. In order to better the ghetto we have to support one another.

In order to move forward we must free ourselves of the pain, hurt and the struggle. It will hurt even more to free ourselves, but it's well worth it. New beginnings aren't easy, but it's better to have a new beginning than to live in the past pain of what was. The story of life is love in growth. Pain can be joy, a struggle can be success, and hate can turn into invisible love. We will never reach joy if we only focus on the pain. We will never reach success if we continue to complain about the struggle. We can't allow hate to interfere with our love. Life is once, don't waste it on nonsense. It's important we know who we are; our history, our strength and our power.

Pursue life and happiness; it's ours once we pursue it with resolve and a steadfast faith. We have our own light, shine yours! We don't have to steal or hate others for what we can accomplish and achieve more of. Let's make the most of life. Even if it is the smallest deed, such as giving a homeless person our loose change or helping someone push their car out the street. A little kindness goes a long way. It's not each other we hate; it's the way of the ghetto we despise. We take our stress out on the wrong people and things.

Self-Pity

We can't pity ourselves because we were born into the ghetto with broken lives. We can't pity ourselves because we were born into poverty, or born a crack baby. We can't pity ourselves because we were born into a race that's hated beyond measurement. We can't pity ourselves and wish we were never born or wish we were dead; we are chosen to be who we are. Having one parent or no parents is not a reason to pity ourselves. We can't pity ourselves because we are orphaned children, living in a shelter, or maybe we lost our childhood. We can't pity ourselves because we have been abused, neglected or abandoned. We can't pity ourselves because we don't have all the up to date clothes, shoes, material things, or finest things in life at this moment.

We can't pity ourselves because we don't have the best food or no money and living as immigrants or prisoners. We can't pity ourselves because we think we're not the most beautiful person on earth on the outside. We can't pity ourselves because the harm others caused us. We can't pity ourselves because we are a stripper. We can't pity ourselves because love and life seems lost. We have no time to sit around and fell sorry for ourselves, spending too much time in our own sorrow we allow valuable time to be wasted. Understand that life is a process that comes day after day. Each day comes with new blessings and miracles when we have faith in God.

Once we put God first and keep Him there everything falls into place. We will eat the good of the land. He will give us the power to make wealth, and protect us on our life journey and mend our broken lives. We can rise to be whoever we're meant to be out of any situation. We can't allow this man-made lie make us live as nobodies and miserable. We've got to get rid of the slave way of thinking and enter into more of a Godly way of thinking. How? With love, faith, peace and harmony with life.

We can't allow the struggles of today ruin our opportunities of success for tomorrow. Life is full of obstacles, but a winner is someone who overcomes. We can't allow the struggle of life to ruin our life before we even have a shot at really living. We don't have to follow the path of another man or woman to be the inner person we are. Failure is not what hurts, never trying is what hurts. We will always have our own footprints; rather or rather not we chose to take our own steps. We can't allow our mothers' or fathers' mistakes keep us from the pursuit of happiness. We can't pity ourselves because of the situations we're born into. We have within us the potential for greatness, self-government and to create a more utopian society.

Our lives are precious and we have a destiny to fulfill. God's love is available for anyone who accepts it. He will always love us no matter who we are or what our pasts consist of. He has already accepted and forgave us long before we knew it. We can't allow ostracism or oppression to overcome us; it sits waiting for an opportunity to devour us. The struggle is nothing but invisible strength that leads to success; only when attention is paid and the necessary steps are made. Life is something like a rollercoaster, at some point the ride must come to an end, we'll get off dizzy but refreshed and ready for whatever.

Don't let the struggle overcome you. We have been denied our liberty and prosperity for too long, we must take ownership of our own lives. We must add some love, intelligence, comfort, and wealth to ourselves and communities. We can't spend our lives chasing a dollar and material values. We must chase our dreams and goals and introduce our souls to our physical bodies. In life we'll make millions of mistakes, but our mistakes don't define us or our character, but more so the decisions we have made. The way we go about correcting our mistakes is what defines our character.

We must learn from past lessons, failures and mistakes, and then we can build a better life from poor judgment. If we don't learn from our past mistakes we will always repeat them. Eliminate poor behavior and judgment. Poor decisions lead to a poor lifestyle. We need to start making smart, wise and rich decisions in a poor society. It doesn't matter the life we live: rich, poor, black, white, ugly, or pretty: we all have a higher power to answer to. It doesn't matter who we are in the eye of man, and it doesn't matter the title we carry; we still answer to a Lord that's above all men. "Wherefore God also hath exalted Him and given Him a name which is above every name: That at the name of Jesus every knee shall bow, of [things] in heaven, and in earth, and under the earth; And every tongue should confess that Jesus Christ [is] Lord, to the glory of God the Father." -Philippians 2: 9-11

Today we are extremely selfish with our love and support. We only think about sex, money, drugs and other things that are not important. "This know also, that in the last days perilous times shall come. For men shall be lovers of their own selves, covetous, boasters, proud, blasphemers, disobedient to parents, unthankful, unholy, without natural affection, trucebreakers, false accusers, incontinent, fierce, despisers of those that are good, traitors, heady, high minded, lovers of pleasure more than lovers of God; having a form of godliness, but denying the power thereof: from such turn away. For of this sort are they which creep into houses, and lead captive silly women laden with sins lead away with divers lusts, ever learning, and never able to come to the knowledge of the truth." -2 Timothy 3: 1.7.

When we learn life is much bigger than just us and our needs the better we will understand, and the easier our journey will be. We are natural born leaders, but chose to follow the path of society and become prisoners, deadbeats, prostitutes, gangsters, or nobodies. I don't really think we understand who we are and how important we are to God, life and to this world.

The only losers are those who accept defeat. We can't allow fear to substitutes our lives. We must live fearless and add some value to our self-worth. Somehow we lost our way because of hurt, pain, struggles, confusion and lies. We try to find every way possible to escape the feeling of emptiness. The only way to escape is to go deep within a broken heart and uncover the buried treasures and strength. The last thing we want to do is spend time alone with ourselves because of the feelings of emptiness and loneliness make us weak to our knees.

The person who is hurting is not our physical being. It's the person inside who is hurting, that's the same person with the healing powers. For some reason we feel the inner person is useless, crazy and weird. That's the person who doesn't fit in with the rest of society and all we want is to be accepted somewhere. So we hide who we are to feel accepted. We keep that part of us isolated because it seems nobody will ever understand the pain of our hearts (at least that's what we think).

The broken spirits and the fears of our souls lead to the confused mind set. Truth be told, we all feel the same way, just hide it behind different faces. In this world we all wear a mask just to get through the day and feel accepted. What's funny to me is how we show no fear in the ghetto but show too much fear toward life. The moment it's time to stand our ground we freeze as if we don't know A from B.

When I say stand our ground, what I mean is in real life, when it's time to face reality, like paying bills, taking care of our children, not selling drugs for excuses and being more independent, achieving our personal greatness. We can't feel sorry for ourselves because of what we were born into, most of America's Presidents or legends came from backgrounds similar to ours, but they had a desire within them. We can't allow man to install fear in us because of whom we think they are. If you don't have anybody to believe in or look up to, believe in yourself and define yourself.

We all have a unique life with our own story that only we have the insight to that needs to be shared. Communicating our life lessons, pain, gifts and talents with others is simply when we believe in ourselves, and want to help others grow with their pain, even with all the skepticism. That's what it means to shine our lights and helping others. We've got plenty to say, share and do, and the world needs to hear and see it in our own unique voices and lives! Why keep hiding our light because of fear and what folks might think?

We can't worry too much about how others are going to take our message; we just got to deliver it with sincerity. No one can't ever accuse us of not having a big heart, because we have a huge one, we just hide and refuse to use and live from it. We have enough room in our hearts for not just those we love, but for anyone who needs us. Our mission now is to help those in that pursuit category to find what they're after without feeling obligated to provide it yourself. In other words, don't try to go out and get them what they need. Guide them toward it instead, with faith.

"Be as proud of your race today as our fathers were in days of yore. We have beautiful history, and we shall create another in the future that will astonish the world." -Marcus Garvey

To be men or women means more than just making money. The life of the streets is a trap; a trap that's almost impossible to get out of. The best way out is never to get in. You ask how are you to feed your family, when the streets are the only pay; I ask how is your family to eat when you're no longer there?

"For we wrestle not against flesh and blood, but against principalities, against powers, against the rulers of the darkness of this world, against spiritual wickedness in high [places]. Wherefore take unto you the whole armour of God, that ye may be able to withstand in the evil day, and having done all, to stand. Stand therefore, having your loins girt about with truth, and having on

the breastplate of righteousness;" **Ephesians 6: 12-14.**

There comes a time in our life when we must call out and answer the call of God. The call of God could be anything, not just preaching behind a pulpit. Why live with no goals? Why go through life with no self-understanding? Why carry yourself and your family through unnecessary hurts; why spend money you don't have to waste?

The life ghetto people live is backward. We gotta turn this around. We gotta strive for victory and personal greatness. We must go after success and not something that's going to get us by day to day. We must leave our children inheritances, not just money or pain, but the value of life, and the history of where we are from, other than the ghetto. We must reach the height of our power as a person and as a race of people. We can no longer allow confusion and poverty to have its way. We've got to find the truth and our way through this madness. Why is it so hard for us to love ourselves and not be our own worst enemy?

Chapter 7 - Predestined before our birth

We have been under attack before birth. We were born into this as infants. We had a fight on our hands before we knew it. The fight is not with each other, it's within. It's a spiritual, mental, culture battle. We have no idea how or why we are caught in a battle. The battle is the Lord's, but the victory is ours! It's because God wants to save our souls and the devil wants us to burn with him (misery loves company), and the U. S. wants us off the face of this earth. We have no idea what is going on or probably don't even care; we don't know what or who we stand for. It's a battle for mankind's life and freedom. Who can control the world the best, man or God?

We were lost the moment we came out the womb. We had no idea what our future held, not knowing what a future was. All we knew was to cry as infants praying somebody would hear and comfort us. As time progressed we grew into children that only wanted our way, not caring about nothing but our wants and thought we knew everything. Most of the time we never got our way, so we grew upset because we wanted our way or wanted somebody to be there to teach us the way in which to go. All along life was still evolving, but we didn't care or pay attention; life was pointless. We never took a moment to give the future a thought, we only cared about now. Nobody told us what life really was or what it meant.

So we grew confused and lost not knowing anything about ourselves but our names and the way we look. All we knew was we had wants, not really caring about our needs, not really understanding our freedom and how we got it. We knew we either had a penis or a vagina, not really understanding the nature behind it; we just like the feeling of using it. So we allowed our genitalia to get us in more trouble than we bargained for. Now, we are at the point where we created life before the age of 21. (A shout out to the teenager girls who are not pregnant.)

We are more confused than ever because we were already lost in our own life, not knowing what was next. So we would do whatever it took to feed our offspring, until one day it all changed for the worse. The life we once created on the seashore washed before our very own eyes. We realized we grew into people we don't even know or understand. We started hating ourselves and cursing the Most High because of no understanding of our own situation. We feel as if we're nothing; we feel worthless and hopeless. So we question ourselves and come up with no answers.

Not knowing we had to build our broken lives on the foundation of Christ and not the shore or on man's words, nor government assistance. *"Whosoever cometh to me, and heareth my sayings, and doeth them, I will shew you to whom he is like: He is like a man which built an house, and digged deep, and laid the foundation on a rock: and when the flood arose, the stream beat vehemently upon that house, and could not shake it: for it was founded upon a rock. But he that heareth, and doeth not, is like a man that without a foundation built an house upon the earth; against which the stream did beat vehemently, and immediately it fell; and the ruin of that house was great."* Luke 6: 47-49.

We had no idea it started before we were conceived. Our minds have been installed with hate, fear and ignorance as we grew, not because we hate or fear others, more so because we hate and fear what we see in the mirror. Not that we don't have or want to show love, but because love is what we fear; but it's what we want or never had. It's something we don't know the meaning of, but think we know all about it. Learn to forgive those who hurt you and forgive yourself, don't commend them; just pray for them. Pray for your family, friends, enemies, and the people who live in your community/world.

"Confess faults one to another, and pray for one another, that ye may be healed. The effective fervent prayer of a righteous man availeth much." James 5: 16

Search

We search for answers everywhere and do a little of everything hoping to get answers, and to find something to fill the void before we collapse from a broken heart. We have so many unanswered questions dying to know why this, why that. We only think about the questions but never seek the answers. So we run from the pieces of a broken heart, too afraid to try to patch the pieces together.

We don't even give ourselves a chance at real life because we fear a blessed life and that's all we want. We think God is not concerned with our problems, but He is (*"Humble yourselves therefore under the mighty hand of God, that he may exalt you in due time: Casting all your care upon him; for he careth for you. Be sober, be vigilant; because your adversary the devil, as a roaring lion, walketh about, seeking whom he may devour: Whom resist stedfast in the faith, knowing that the same afflictions are accomplished in your brethren that are in the world. But the God of all grace, who hath called us unto His eternal glory by Christ Jesus, after that ye have suffered a while, make you perfect, stablish, strengthen, settle [you]. To Him [be] glory and dominion forever and ever. Amen."* (1 Peter 5: 6-11).

We are so confused in our minds we struggle to put the pieces together and sometimes we don't even try. The way of man has messed up our minds, so we need to organize our life in our mind to make our reality better.

"My people are destroyed for lack of knowledge: because thou hast rejected knowledge, I will also reject thee, that thou shalt be no priest to me: seeing thou hast forgotten the law of thy God, I will also forget thy children." -Hosea 4: 6.

We no longer seek the truth so if we don't seek the truth, what do we seek? The world has become so scientific that the people think we're becoming more powerful than GOD. Let me remind you, God is the Creator of all things ("In t*he beginning was the Word, and the Word was with God, and the Word was God. 2 The same was in the beginning with God. 3 All things were made by him; and without him was not anything made that was made. 4 In him was life; and the life was the light of men. 5 And the light shineth in darkness; and the darkness comprehended it not."* -John 1: 1-5)

We have no power compared to the power of God; His Word is everything. The world's ignorance has cast God out of the photo and now the picture of life has no art. God only wants our souls to be forever in His presence, in peace, and for our life here on earth to be enjoyed. "For God so loved the world that He gave His only begotten son that whoever believeth in Him should not perish, but have everlasting life." -John 3: 16

When the devil attacks us he aims at our hearts, consciousness, souls, spirits, physical bodies and at times our finances, with heart-rending bad decisions, pain in our souls, broken spirits and diseases in our bodies. *"3He healeth the broken in heart, and bindeth up their wounds. 4 He telleth the number of the stars; He calleth them all by [their] names. 5 Great [is] our Lord, and of great power: His understanding [is] infinite."* Psalms 147: 3-5.

The devil uses fear, greed and hate to destroy us from ourselves. The U. S. uses us to stop our own progress. God uses faith, love and prosperity to help build us for our life; only when we choose to accept His guidance. We need to say forget the petty things, and evaluate our minds to evaluate our lives and pockets. It's so easy for a person to lose and throw away their life.

It's so easy for some of us to take a person's life and not understand the pain we cause. Every crime is pointless and could have been prevented. We act as if we can't make a wise decision to save our own lives. We don't pursue life, we don't educate our brains and we don't feed our spirits with the guidance we search for. We need to pursue life, educate our minds and allow the Holy Spirit to guide us in our hearts.

Some only want to dress our bodies with designer clothes, get our hair done and think life is about money, drugs, clothes and sex. We confuse ourselves with material things and life. What were humans wearing before high fashion? How was the world living/traveling before oil? How were we communicating before technology? What will we do when or if it fails? We think it's going to last forever, but life is changing and our valuable resources are running low. Everything has advanced other than the African American culture. We look everywhere to find answers and comfort others than inside a broken heart. We are afraid to call out to God because we strive to be super human, and think we can take care of everything by ourselves; but we're not and we can't. We curse others by punishing ourselves and feeling sorry for ourselves.

People and life need our gifts, dreams, hope, ideas, love and leadership. There's enough people living nightmares and we don't need to be one more of those people. There's a hero inside us all, if we look inside our hearts. There are answers to so many unanswered questions if we reach into our souls and do some soul searching. We can bring the hero out of us and the sorrow will release itself, and the fear will flee from our lives. We have the strength to prevail, but we feel hope is dead. It's not that hope is dead but we have to bring hope alive. Hope never died. It's just that most of us never gave birth to our own potential. We are so worried about what we can't do, that we don't realize what we can do. Why does it seem so much easier for us to believe in bad fortune, but so much more difficult to trust in our good fortune?

Those are the main questions most of us are facing right now. We have great potential, but in order for us to really live it through, we need to believe not only that we have it, but that the universe wants to see us shine. We just can't question our surroundings, we must question ourselves too.

We must push ourselves out our comfort zones. We need to push beyond our own boundaries, and identify with the universal source which is God. A part of God lives inside each of us believers and non-believers. We just never live for ourselves, our lives, love, hopes, dreams, freedom are GOD'S love. We live for a selfish America dollar, leaving ourselves and others in the darkness to please who and what? If only we wake up before it's too late we will do great deeds. We struggle with this because we don't know who we are and what we stand for. Every man has a purpose. Trust that you have a purpose in this world that welcomes your gifts of awareness and altruistic visions.

We are the children of God and we stand for His glory. We don't know what He wants, but He only wants to love us and supply all our needs, spiritually, mentally, physically, and financially. ("But my God shall supply all your needs according to his riches and glories in Christ Jesus." -Philippians 4: 19) We don't know that because we depend on a dollar and the government for everything, and that's where we go wrong. We don't know the only true enemy we have is the devil and the greed of the U. S. A. government/people. Everything we do and have depends on Mother Nature, food, water and oxygen for the body, land for our homes and streets to drive our cars, and much more. Mother Nature is something that's not man-made. Who created our bodies to depend on food, water and oxygen? Who created the land to build our houses? Who provide space for internet? Man didn't! If we have a Mother Nature then we must have a Heavenly Father.

Help

We rather harm one another than offer a helping hand, shut up, rather than speak up, say goodbye than say hello, and take a seat than take a stand. It's easy to live in the past, and that's where we prefer to be while letting the moments of our lives slip by, forgetting about our future. Settling for less is easier than creating more; so is living in the shadows than letting our own lights shine. We'd rather follow than lead. I think one of our main problems is we substitute who we are because then we don't have to have a sense of accountability. If we continue to fall back then the responsibility is always put on someone else.

We feel as if we be ourselves we won't be accepted into a lost society. Truth be told everybody in society is pretending to be what they are, not to feel comfortable and accepted. We were born with a broken heart but never acknowledged it because poverty, pain and being ignorant to the truth blinds us, so we just go wherever society goes.

From time after time we have been searching for wholeness, because of the feeling of emptiness and being incomplete. We lost ourselves before we could discover who we were, and that's the cycle of the ghetto until it's broken. The ghetto's streets have its own personality which is more of a lie; which the average ghetto person wants to be, just to feel like a real person. Our life is surrounded by façades; feeling broken on the inside but the outside is showing a different person, trying to cover the hurt, shame and lies.

The truth is something we people know, but run from because of the fear to face what hurts the most. The truth shall set us free indeed, but it will hurt. We must find the truth because the lies hurt just as much as the truth does. We weren't sent here to be broken. Though we know that we will have to experience pain during our lifetimes, we should use that are reasons to help one another. We came here to help build the broken. Everyone experiences pain, just like John 16: 33 says: "These things I've spoken unto you that in me [Jesus] you will have peace. In the world you will have tribulations, but be of good cheer, I have overcome the world."

We don't know this because we don't know who we are, we are not of man and we were never meant to live the life man created. We think we own the world but we don't. We were born with nothing and we will die with nothing.

We have to set our souls free and open our hearts to the Spirit of God, and quit being selfish. We always want something and never want to give anything. I guess you say what's to give when nothing was given and we're still suffering, right? That's not the point. The Bible tells us to "Give, and it shall come back to you. Good measure, pressed down, shaken together and running over shall men give into your bosom. For with the same measure that you mete withal it shall be measured to you again," Luke 6: 38. Once we unite and restore our communities, faith and families we will be greater than before. Power is in the people. Together, we are strong; divided, we are weak and vulnerable to failure. We always want something and never want to give anything.

There are people who always complain when there is nothing to complain about. They always want the truth but always lie. They always want to explore the world but don't leave the block. They complain about the food they eat when folks are starving. They only pay attention to rap videos, sports, the latest trends and the latest gossip, but pay life little attention. We all want to be loved but show no love. We all want to be accepted but don't want to accept others. We all want to be respected but show no respect. We all want to be heard but don't take time to listen.

Desiring to want to blow up and show up is useless if we don't grow up. We all want to be seen but won't take a moment to open our own eyes. We are so quick to walk away and giving up on ourselves and don't want to use our strength to become who we are meant to be. We want our blessings but curse other folks' lives. Sometimes the ghetto life doesn't seem real, buts it's all too real. What is this we are living? Would somebody tell me? We all want to make our journey through life, but don't want to take the necessary steps toward wholeness.

So many questions, but no answers; is it because we never verbally ask the questions? Start asking those serious questions; you won't look stupid. We need to stop preparing for the worst in the darkness of our lives and started focusing on a better outcome. We can't allow fear to kill our faith. This life and the decisions we make we are responsible for. Life is truly one of the greatest gifts man can ever receive, and I don't think we truly understand the meaning of life. Life is so important Christ gave His life all for mankind, it's that important.

GOD has given us love, power and a sound mind (2 Timothy 1: 7), goals, dreams, ideas and gifts that are important to our lives and the lives of those on planet earth. Only if people knew Satan is our only enemy as a human race. He makes us enemies with each other with lies, stupidity, greed, deceiving our minds, and making us feel worthless to life and God's Will. His goal is to keep us from the love of God in any and every way possible. He wants our lives to be miserable. ("Be sober, be vigilant; because your adversary the devil is, is as a roaring lion, walketh around, seeking whom he mayeth devour," 1 Peter 5: 8) It's like the devil and the government of U. S. A are working together to hold us back. They don't want us to use our ideas, gifts, talents, dreams; our goals or our love to heal the world as a whole.

Innocent people being killed in wars, people suffering from poverty, that's not God doing that, but man's greed and selfishness. We blame God for all the bad things when we're the ones being disobedient. We make ourselves pointless by not obeying. We must understand God has great love for us, and a purpose for our lives. Only when we are willing to pursue life we start to understand how life and God's love and graces works. We must understand fear and money is a tool they use to keep us from happiness and make us think we can't achieve something.

The enemy's goal is to destroy the children of God, and keep us away from the glory of Heaven's Kingdom. They use all their power to kill our faith in God and to turn our backs on God Almighty. The system is the reason we have so much doubt, poverty, and pain and cause harm to ourselves and others. The way we can let go of pain, or whatever is holding us back is to turn back to the Creator and share love in a hated place, and shed light on the dark. Only if we knew the life we're supposed to live here on earth, we wouldn't follow the path of a lost mankind.

We would help mankind acknowledge God, The Missing Piece. We would take our personal paths which were set for us before birth. We wouldn't sell ourselves short of life because of pain, fear, hurt, struggle or other things that keep us from progression. Really nothing stops us, we keep ourselves hostage. Life continues through it all. It's really up to us to move forward. Why must we allow our children to see us destroy ourselves and their futures? Why must we scar them at such an early age?

Chapter 8 – The power to Rise

"Black people have always been in America's wilderness in search of a promised land." -Cornel West

We have the willpower to rise above all of this hate and useless minutia that really serves us no purpose. Some pain is temporary but it will stay a lifetime if we keep it company. Some pains are growing pains, and will continue as we better ourselves. Once we wake up from the European American dream and realize we're living the American nightmare, then we can progress. Living our personal dreams leads to the American dream. All we have as ghetto Americans is our dreams, and even that they want to take. We will always have a million interruptions, but that's because without them we will never know our strength, power, or identity.

They never wanted us to find or know our identity, power, history or strength, and never wanted us to have unity as a race. That's why they want to keep us under their control and divide us. We must overcome! We must understand that they don't hate us because of our skin color, but because of our true identity and character. If we, as a culture of people, would stand together and stand our ground we would be a world movement and we would rule again! If we, as a culture of people, was to find or discover our personal strength and power we would rule ourselves.

That's what they fear! They don't hate us because of the things we do to each other, but more so of the things we could do for each other. We must open our minds to life and let the hate devour itself. They don't put us in jail because that's where we belong, but because they want to control our lives. We would work a 9-5 for a lifetime if we could get a job. Based on information given by people who are prisoners and from this resource, *http: //ezinearticles. com/? How-Much-Money-Do-Prisoners-Make? &id=4452183*,

prisoners are paid pennies to do the same labor a free man is paid much more in dollars per hour. Their pay goes from .014 cents per hour to somewhere under 2.00 dollars.

They give us guns, not for our protection, but for us to kill each other without getting the dirt on their hands. They give us drugs, not for our pain, but to destroy ourselves. Therefore, they kill two or more birds with one stone. They don't want us to live, but want us six feet beneath mother earth. If they gave us a fair shot at life they would be fearful of the fact that it's possible we would rise above them, and live to our full integrity. The thing is they know we want the same things they do and we want them to quit impoverishing our communities.

We want nothing more than our freedom, which we think we have. We want them to quit with the lies in the texts books and put the truth in our books, and to stop deceiving our people's minds. We can make it possible. The fear they have of us is why they want to keep us under their control. We have to protect our lives by protecting our minds and the decisions we make. The future of us and our culture depends heavily on this generation and one another. They think we are a group of stupid and lazy niggers. We have to show them how intelligent we are, because some of us dropped out of school doesn't make us stupid or useless. We still have a higher purpose to serve, that goes beyond our imagination.

What makes you think they are going to give an average black person like me or you anything? African Americans have always been on a spiritual journey to freedom, God has always been directing our paths. Our ghettos are at the red sea and the sea hasn't begun to part until we start to step across. This is either a new era for the ghetto people or the fall back into enemies' hands. We have to refuse to give up. We have the ability to look at the past (slavery) and the future (presidency). We came from the lowest of the low, to the highest of the high; that shows the strength of our people. We have to choose. We have decisions to make; we're at a crossing point. We have to make wise and smart choices and be able to trust our decisions and the power of our instincts. Most Europeans only wanted power, wealth, land and control. We have to look beyond that in order to rise.

Chapter 9 - The Ghetto

"Hungry men have no respect for law, authority or human life."
-Marcus Garvey

Understand the word ghetto is not just for black people. Merriam-Webster online dictionary defines it as: a quarter of a city in which members of a minority group live especially because of social, legal, or economic pressure. In my opinion, it's a community of misunderstood people, a group of people that the system calls nobodies, a group of people intimidate by the system. Ghetto is a community of rebels lost on who they are and where they are. It is a place where families suffer in sorrow and in desperate need of help and each other's support. It is a community of people who's been suffering from poverty and distress since the birth of a great nation. It is a community of people who live in the enemies' hands and won't support each other and became each other's' enemies.

An American ghetto to me is any community that lives below the poverty line, poor, poverty stricken, a destitute and impoverished people. A Community filled with silent hope; a community of people that don't know what's coming next. A community of individuals who are selfish, and have nowhere else to go. A community of hungry people who are broken by the system of America and have little care for anything. A community of people who wants justice, peace, liberty, the pursuit of happiness and equal opportunities, but don't want to pursue it. America is a multiracial nation of people: it's Black, White, Asian, Latino, Native American, Mexican, Indian, and anybody who wants to pursue happiness or a better way of life. Why do you think so many people want to live in America?

Why must we force ourselves into believing lies? Why won't we accept the truth? Why must we make each other mothers/

families cry? Are we our brothers' & sisters' keepers, or are we what keeps bringing jinx to our brothers and sisters? Why must we allow the system to manipulate us? By us being ignorant to the system and only paying attention to the streets we are giving the system time and the ability to destroy us. What's so hard about being grown? Is it because we always wanted to be grown as a child and now that we are grown we want to be kids again? Why must we live in such a rush? Why must we believe we are something we weren't intended to be by becoming felons, prostitutes, babies' daddies, babies' mamas, criminals, statistics, strippers, gangsters, pimps or drug dealers? Why must our own mind set destroy us?

For if a man think himself to be something, when he is nothing, he deceiveth himself.

But let every man prove his own work, and then shall he have rejoicing in himself alone, and not in another. For every man shall bear his own burden.

Let him that is taught in the word communicate unto him that teacheth in all good things. -Galatians 6: 3-6.

Why does it seem like some of our role models are rappers, athletes, porn stars and drug dealers? Most of them are in and out of jail; doesn't that tell you that their paths might not be the right way? If drugs and ignorance divides us, what holds us together? Why must our children want to be so grown before their time? Why do we wait until it's too late to listen and make changes? Why won't we listen to that voice within our hearts? Every day that we worry about pulling licks, killing, and running the streets is another day lost. Why must we allow the streets to take us alive? Why must we argue/fight with each other over nothing, but won't argue/fight for our rights and freedom? Why must we be a part of the problem and not the solution? Our ignorance, selfishness and fears are gold to the Europeans' empire, where as their greed, arrogance and authority is misery to us.

> *"Black people are inferior to white men and we must forever govern them."* -Abraham Lincoln

They enjoy their empire being unquestioned and not challenged. Why don't we question and challenge them? Are we afraid? They are looking to subdue and conquer us ghetto people and we help them in ways we can't even understand. When we answer these questions with open minds and common sense we can start to understand the steps we must take to overcome self-hostage and conspiracy. If you want to overcome poverty, ignorance and pain, we must have faith and be determine to believe, then we will overcome and succeed in whatever our desires and accomplishments maybe. A negative mindset and attitude will help us get nowhere and achieve nothing in this world or life. Anyone who has the determination, willpower, solid faith in God and in him/herself and stick to their purpose can achieve greatness; don't expect to achieve without trials and tests.

> *"Champions aren't made in the gyms. Champions are made from something they have deep inside them - a desire, a dream, and a vision."* Muhammad Ali

A true American is anybody who steps out the shadows and creates life, peace, justice, liberty and prosperity for all people; who accepts and gives the love of God. Life is about personal growth & development, but not without self-understanding and love. Because we were born in the ghetto doesn't mean we don't matter or can't make a difference. Understand, God is a God of justice and He is fair. We cause life to be unfair with the way we treat each other. just mainly They could care less about the American people's lives; they just want sovereign power. Our life is in our hands, life is up to us. We must pursue happiness for ourselves, families and our communities. The only thing a person is going to give us is love or hate, happiness or misery, the truth or a lie. It's up to us what we accept.

I know it's hard to have faith and live up to our potential and do good deeds in a poor, ignorant society, but we still have to be the best we can while others are being the worst at themselves. We can't allow others' ignorance to slow our progress. We need to renew ourselves spiritually and mentally by visualizing the life we want to live and moving with faith in that direction. Constantly reminding ourselves of the promise of God in our minds and hearts and keeping it. The constant struggle to measure up to God's level and His will for our life is the only thing on earth that can make life great, beautiful and fruitful. Remember, the heart and mind is the foundation to the structure of the life we build. Our hearts and minds are our soil to life and the seeds we plant soon become our reality. Only we people in the ghetto truly know our situations and only we can improve it. *"For as he thinketh in his heart, so [is] he…" –Proverbs 23: 7*

"There is not a Black America and a White America and Latino America and Asian America; there's the United States of America."
– President Barack Obama.

Chapter 10 – The Enemy's Conversation

"No matter what they took from us, they shouldn't be able to take our faith, dignity, unity are courage... The soul that is within us no man can degrade." -Frederick Douglass

They said let them suffer and die. They said they'll never make it out the ghetto. They said let's make it impossible for those people to live. They said let's give them drugs and guns and make them slave babies war on each other, and make laws against drugs and guns. Let's keep them in our control. They said let's break them and their families, and keep their lives shattered.

They said let's come up with an ingenious system and the strength and weakness of the system will be them. They will never know because they are too lazy to figure it all out and too scared to speak up. They said let's make them hate each other over the American dollar. Let's make them chase a dollar that will come back to us, and take their lives while they are rushing to keep up with nothing. Let's make it so the kids feel they don't need school and drop out; let's make their role models be the dope boys. Let's take their focus off the Almighty God; therefore, they won't be able to find their way through life. Confusion comes easy when they're confined in the ghetto mind-frame. Let's show them our rich and beautiful life from afar but keep it in their face. Let's make them envy our lives.

Making them hate themselves and their neighbors but love our wealth is worth it to keep them in their place. Let's make it hard for them to believe and make them feel their dreams can never be accomplished. Let's keep them in a difficult struggle from day to day. Let's keep them blind to the truth but keep the truth right in their faces. Let's make them forget where they came from, so they won't know where they are headed. Let's keep them in the mind-frame of slaves but make them think they are free, cursing themselves and being strangers to each other, even though they are relatives. Let's keep them away from their true identities and make it so that everything they need they steal. We'll make it so they do more harm to themselves than the KKK did to them. Let's make them curse their offspring, generation after generation. Let's keep America strong by keeping them weak to our system. Let's break them down from who they are, and make them who we want them to be.

Convincing them that we are for them but we are their worst enemy is easy when they are against each other. Let's take everything from them so they fear, rob, and kill each other. Let's make and break them by not allowing them to build themselves. Let's make them live a false life. Why not sit back and enjoy life while their culture self-destructs and their lives are miserable. Let's give them their freedom and watch them act like baboons and niggers and do nothing with it but give it back. Let's laugh at the American idiots!

"These Negroes, they're getting pretty uppity these days and that's a problem for us since they've got something now they never had before; the political pull to back up their uppityness. Now we've got to do something about this, we've got to give them a little something, just enough to quiet them down, not enough to make a difference..." -Sen. Lyndon B. Johnson

Their system violates our livelihood but the moment we engage to excel violates their laws, then they want to put us in prison. The Europeans are following the path that's been laid for them. They've been misguiding us for centuries, but now let's allow God to guide us again. They seem to judge everything we do as African Americans as wrong and a crime, from how we wear our clothes to our music. We have no independence. Why is there a war on how we wear our clothes and our music but no war on poverty?

"We gotta realize we gotta problem, And the government? The only time they care, is election time, And they seem to think the only solution is, Build more prisons to throw us in..... it's not right, We got homies dyin' over nothing" –Silkk the Shocker

Chapter 11 - Our Broken Hearts

"I am the American heartbreak! The rock on which freedom stumped its toe." -Langston Hughes

Our hearts are broken because our culture is broken; we were born into broken lives that have never been fixed. We never had love from our parents because our parents are deceased or they just never been there. Our hearts are broken because we can't find a reason to love ourselves from within, but we feel as if we can love another human. If we can't love ourselves how can we love another soul?

Our hearts are broken because it seems as if we can't find wholeness within or outside ourselves. Our hearts are crying but nobody hears our silent cries; we don't give ourselves the whole 100%. Our hearts are broken not because of hate or pain, but because we have nothing but love and can't share or express it, or folks won't accept it. We desire to be loved, we need to be loved, or folks use our love as a weapon against us. We make our love invisible toward life. Our hearts is broken because we know we must stand our ground, but fear has its hold. *"For God hath not given us the spirit of fear, but of love, power and of a sound mind."* -2 Timothy1: 7.

Our hearts are broken because we feel our lives are pointless because we have nothing, nobody and no cash. It's the opposite way around, once we started building our lives then help somehow comes along out the blue. We want to ask for help but afraid somebody will say "I told you," or we don't have a soul to count on. That's why it's important to be self-reliant. We lost our way chasing insufficient objects.

Our hearts are broken because we are in debt with Christ and we owe Him our allegiance, but feel He won't accept us because all the dirty things we have done. He accepted us any way we come, as long we come. Our hearts are broken because life's heart is broken and it's going to take us all to do our personal part to patch the pieces back together. We need to stop putting ourselves in situations our hearts and our lives can't handle. We will never outgrow the warfare in our lives, but as we progress we will become great warriors of faith.

As long as we have God we can go on and go inside our broken hearts and mend the piece as we progress. We can't allow a broken heart to devour our lives. A broken heart fixes itself once we allow God to work His miracles through us. We must keep our minds and hearts in the protection of God and allow Him to lead. *"But this the covenant that I will make the house of Israel; After those days, saith the Lord, I will put my law in their inward parts, and write it in their hearts; and will be their God, and they shall be my people."* -Jeremiah 31: 33

He knows and feels our pain; and at times I wonder if we feel His pain. It hurts Him to know He gave His children the power to overcome the enemies' tricks, but we allow them to defeat our faith and cause our lives to be miserable. Our hearts are broken because we're fearful of what's promised to us. The promise of GOD! We're afraid of the pursuit because we don't know the outcome. Why? Our future depends on if we let go of all our baggage, including anyone and anything that holds us back from moving toward the opportunities that awaits us. We have to get this show on the road with a confident attitude and a grateful heart. We can mend our broken hearts once we start loving ourselves for who we are. We can't fully love ourselves until we love God. *"Delight thyself also in the Lord; and He shall give thee the desires of thine heart."* -Psalms 37: 4

We have carried the guilt, the shame and the anger for too long; we have kept the wounds of our scars opened for too long. Time has come for us to let go and heal. We have to keep, learn and teach from the lessons we were taught and move on with life and heal.

"Even if we don't admit it, sometimes in the back of our minds we really want to fall down and cry and never get up, but we gotta get up 'cause we gotta pay bills and take care of our children, even though we feel like losers, but we ain't no losers; we're God's children and can't nothing move us." -Lyfe Jennings

Chapter 12 – GOD

"I love to think of nature as an unlimited broadcasting station, through which God speaks to us every hour, if we will only tune in." -George Washington Carver

God loves us all, we are His creation; our dreams are His dreams, our desires are what God wants for our lives. We can only be complete by making Him the instructor. He hears the silence, He hears our voices, and He hears our prayers. He hears our roar; He hears our cries that nobody else notices. He knows who we are; He knows where we are, where we've been and where we're headed. He knows what we've done and what we've been through over the years. He knows our secrets. HE KNOWS ALL! There is nothing we can hide from the Almighty God. We can either trust Him or doubt Him; either way His Word will always prevail. We must accept His love and His care and allow Him to guide our lives through Christ Jesus.

He loves us dearly and the only thing He wants to take care of everything from our mental, physical, spiritual, and financial needs. We know He wants to guide our lives but we're afraid of what people have to say. Little do we know, the folks who are always criticizing us are the same folks who need our faith and need God's grace. They may not admit it, but trust, they do; we all do. We want to make changes in our lives but have been reluctant to do so.

God is the answer we have always been searching for. He is the love we're missing and the missing link to life. He is always on time, even when He is late on our watch; that's because His timing is not our timing and He'll never leave nor forsake His children. Just know He is always there. It doesn't matter the case or situation. He is the beginning and the end; He raises and sets the sun.

He is the breath to life. He sent His son into the world not to save just us, but the world as a whole. "For God so loved the world that He gave His only begotten son, that whosoever shall believeth in Him shall not perish, but shall have everlasting life." -John 3: 16 Allow Him to be your strength, friend, Father and whatever else you need. When God looks at us He don't see what we have or don't have, but He looks at the progress we make spiritually, mentally and our moral growth. He sees what we can be; He sees His best creation. Allow Him to guide you from wherever you are in your life, from lost to found, blind to sight, poverty to plenty.

God is not a joke. There is a God and He is able and alive. He is the source of all things. "A father of the fatherless; and a judge to the widows, God is his only habitation. God setteth the solitary in families: He bringeth out those who are bound with chains: but the rebellious dwell in a dry [land]." -Psalms 68: 5-6

Don't wait until you get a check in the mail to thank God. Don't wait until you lose a dear one, or lose everything to cry out to God, "why me?" Don't wait until judgment day to repent and forgive. God hates sin, not the sinner. People will always say what God is and what God isn't. We have to find out who and what God is to us as individuals.

The Bible, the Word of God, is here to teach us which way to go. The Word of God is to help us free our minds, hearts and spirits to help us grow and heal our brokenness. The Word is for us to take the limits off of God and off ourselves that man placed on us. God said *"delight yourself in the lord and He will give us the desires of our hearts."* Psalms 37: 4

Don't matter what our desires are: a happy family, a successful life, to achieve greatness; take heed to His words and try Him. The Word states that we reap what we sow; our words, thoughts and actions all have a harvest because they once were seeds. Everything we do have results whether it's good or bad. The things we do and the decisions we make have an eternal influence on our life. There's nothing that can explain the horrible misery and suffering that exist in the world today, but hate and love of money. There is no excuse why us, the children of God, should be harassed, tormented and worried; or living in distressful situations, driven to early graves because of the love for money and poverty stricken misery.

Why do we live such miserable existences if the cattle on a thousand hills and all the silver and gold in the world and everything in it belong to the God? I think because we think God doesn't care about us, our needs, or desires. So we don't claim all He says we can have because we have little faith or no faith in Him. God said all that He has is ours, just claim it in His holy name, and don't forget it was the Lord's, our God, who has granted us the power to have wealth. *"But thou shalt remember the Lord thy God for He that giveth thee power to get wealth, that He may establish His covenant which He sware unto thy fathers as this day."* -Deuteronomy 8: 18

Why not accept it?

We should know that God never intended for us to be poor. Man's government is the reason we live such distressful lives; it's not God's kingdom, because God promises to supply all our needs according to His glory through Christ Jesus.

"The spoken word is stronger than the strongest man, Carries the whole world like the strongest hand, through the trials and tribulations you neva let us down JESUS!" -DMX

Chapter 13- Lost and Found

"Some people hear their own inner voices with great clearness and they live by what they hear. Such people become crazy, or they become legends...." –One Stab

When you're lost on the outside you haveto turn to the inside. When your brain can no longer think or carry you, allow your heart to pick you up from where your brain left you adjourn. That means it's time for a new way of thinking, a new way of life. There is a voice inside of us that seems useless to us. Truth is, that's the voice of guidance, self-love and self-worth. That voice wants to guide us to a place we're fearful of going; the unknown bright future. We want to get to that place of wholeness but can't find the strength within to pull ourselves together to get there.

We have the strength and the power but refuse to use it. That voice will never go anywhere until we speak and live from that voice, nor will it steer us wrong. But because we feel we know everything we ignore that voice until a point comes and we wish we would have listened. This the point when it's out of our control and we can no longer carry on the same way; when life is forcing us to take a new route. When we feel as if we can no longer carry on and we want to give up. It means it's time we spread those wings we are fearful of using. There is going to come a time when we must free our spirits to fly on to find strength from the universe. Whoever said we can't fly? Along with R. Kelly, "I believe we can fly. I believe we can touch the sky, We think about it every night and day, We must spread our wings and fly high above the deep valley that seemed so low once a point of time."

The voice within is sometimes scary to listen to, because it seems as if that voice speaks the impossible. That makes us feel crazy and out of our character. Truth is, we must overcome our fears of ourselves and realize we are demigods with limited powers and understanding. We must realize that that's voice is the voice of an Angel, the Holy Spirit trying to guide our physical bodies through life's journey. *"It is the Spirit that quickeneth; the flesh profiteth nothing: the words that I speak unto you are spirit and are life."* -John 6: 63

It's hard to listen because we always want to be able to predict the outcome. When we can't predict the outcome we lose our minds because we hate taking risks on the unknown. That voice wants to teach us that we can trust and believe in ourselves. That voice means us no harm. We harm ourselves when we don't listen and later on wish we would have listened. That voice calls us to believe in ourselves which calls us to believe in a Higher Power.

Good old Times

We sit around and look at old pictures and reminisce on old times, amazed at how fast time flew by knowing that fact, but we ignored it. Looking at the smiles on the faces of families, friends and remembering the good and the bad times we shared gives us a sense of sadness, happiness, and hope and we mesmerize on what was. Wishing it was still the same way as old times. Wishing we could rewind time, but time is irreplaceable. The saddest part about it is it will never be the same, even when we get our second chance at whatever we failed at the first time. It will never be the same as it once was. We can either make it better or worse the next opportunity we get. However, we must go on, and remember the good and bad times we once shared and pray for greater times to come. A strong belief of why we can't move forward is because we are stuck on what was, and what everybody else expects of us.

We try our hardest to get things back the way it was, and it will never be again. We can't picture what is, or what could be, because our minds are stuck on a past life. Continually focusing on what used to be. Can't quite figure how or where it went wrong. Can't understand how we got to this point, and don't know how to get to the next point; feeling so lost asking how could this be. Asking ourselves how could my life come to this? Saying this is not supposed to happen to me; telling ourselves only if we knew what we know now the things we'd do over. Well, we know what we know now, so we can move on forward with the knowledge we learned from the past lessons, and apply them to future life situations. What's crazy is to know we must go on, or get left behind; not by people, but by life, and not change our mindset. Life moves at a pace that's hard to keep up with. At times it may feel as if we can't go on, but we can we have to.

We have so many greater memories to make. We still have our prints to place here on this earth. We can go on. We can start all over again. We can smile, we have many reasons to. We can't continue trying to find things to distract whatever it is we're trying to avoid. That will lead to a pattern of life of trying to hide from our fears, thinking we can't conquer. We must confront our fears and move past those self-imposed limits in our lives. We can hide, run, or hold it all inside, but if we don't face it, it will lead to a miserable life.

Someday we'll figure it all out and move on with life. We just can't wait a lifetime to confront the blockage of progress. Time is the only valuable inheritance we have and we'll never know how long it'll last. Time comes with self-defeat or self-victory. A new beginning is always a new sunshine and a new way of life. We as people confine ourselves to one way of thinking and living. We act as if we are afraid of opening our minds and hearts to a different way of life other than rap, sports, entertainment or drugs.

In the ghetto we confine ourselves to only one way of thinking and living. We feel worthless if we can't rap, play football or basketball so we sell drugs and carry a gun to feel as if we are somebody. Females feel worthless just because of what someone says about them and only want to be a baby mama, and would do anything to get a nigga or keep one. People would do anything for a dollar, even if it means going against his/her best friend or family. Our mentality is messed up, so is our trust in each other. Rap, football, and basketball are not our only talents. Drugs are just an easy escape to the U. S. jail or grave. We have gifts, talents, abilities and ideas we don't even know we have because we don't try.

That's because we don't use our gifts and talents, we think we could get by, by being a follower. We have and can use our personal gifts to get ahead of whatever and be successful. We feel worthless if we can't leave the hood, we don't have to leave the hood to have a beautiful life. We just have to be better ourselves and our communities right where we live and quit being each other's enemies over nothing. We've got to stop thinking we are better than them, or we think they are better than us. Neither of us is better, we're all trying to overcome a similar situation. We must evaluate our minds, find our strength and embrace it. We can't allow the American system to have us victims to our minds and lives and make us want to escape the ghetto.

America don't give us the 100% truth of our history, so it makes a black person seem useless, but it's black people who help shape the country. We must discover the truth for ourselves. They reveal to us what they want us to know, show us what they want us to see and tell us what they want us to hear. We must understand the crisis we were born into, from slavery to the Emancipation, to the failure of the Reconstruction straight to Jim Crow and from the Jim Crow laws straight to the Ghetto. We were born in the middle of the American promise of reconstruction which never happened and as we grew older we fell deeper into the hole, because we refuse to educate ourselves on how we got into this situation and how we can get out. We were born to rise, but because we seek money, sex and material values we lose our way. (*"But seek ye first the Kingdom of God and His righteousness; and all these things shall be added unto you."* -Matthew 6: 33

In the Beginning

We all were born alone at different times for different reason. "To everything there is a season, and a time to every purpose under heaven." -Ecclesiastes 3:1 God ordained these days for us to be born, He put us on this planet for His divine reasons; He has plans. "Before I formed thee in the belly I knew thee; and before thou camest forth out of the womb I sanctified thee…" -Jeremiah 1:5 We stand as Americans with a life purpose. We represent not just ourselves but each other because we are one. Years after birth I realized that we are more than just people who were born poor in the ghetto. I realized we are rich people born into poor sinsituations.

I realized the word ghetto is only use to describe people, their living conditions and their attitudes toward life. To me we can always change our lives if we chose to. Nobody else will and can't do it for us. If you were to look up the word ghetto in Merriam-Webster on line dictionary, you would read this: "A section of a city occupied by a minority group who live there especially because of social, economic, or legal pressure.

What is the ghetto restricted from? We restrict ourselves from truth, life, freedom and the strength of ourselves. Why? Because we allow man to determine our destiny and we chose to follower others. See, the thing is we are restricted from nothing other than man's way. The journey of happiness and wholeness begins with oneself overcoming self-fears and man's so-called limits. The first steps lead to the path we take; rather it's being a prisoner, a president, a baby mama, or the first lady. We must be careful of the directions we chose to take, because at times our own sense of directions leads us to dead ends. I tell you this, if we allow God to direct our paths then we will never run into a dead end, that's a promise.

As life progresses I come to understand that fear and excuses are the only thing that holds us back from accomplishing our dreams and goals and pursuing our purpose. We can't be afraid to fail; if we don't try we have already failed at ourselves and at life. There's nothing to fear but fear. What is fear? The enemy of faith! Years later we stand with a lost generation. I always wondered why we stood ahead and apart from our people. The thing I found out was we never stood apart from our people but ahead as leaders, never a follower unless we are following Christ of course.

What I don't get about our people is how we chose to live the life someone who don't even know us choose for us. We are living the dream of other people and don't even realize it. We hate each other and we have no reason to. Our lives fell beneath the earth's surface but our physical bodies walk solid ground. Why do we pretend to be happy and walk with our heads to the sky but in reality our faces are to the ground? As if our hearts are never sure of the life we live. Is it the fact we try to find comfort in uncomfortable situations? Is it that we are lost in our minds and can't find peace within ourselves?

Is it the fact we don't know who we are, or is it the fact that we run from the person we know deep in our hearts we are, but can't become or don't know how to face that person, although we live with that person day and night, and can't find the path to discovering that person.

"For I delight in the law of God after the inward man: But I see another law in my members, warring against the law of my mind, and bringing me into captivity to the law of sin which is in my members. O wretched man that I am! Who shall deliver me from the body of this death?" Romans 7: 22-24

What is this so-called fear? Is it the feeling of perplexity? Is it the fact of having one way of thinking and being closed minded toward life? Is it the fact our flesh is weak? Is it the self-imprisonment we find ourselves guilty of? We are persecuted but not left without breath. We are thrown down, but not destroyed. We endure so that the Holy Spirit may be made manifest in our lives and bodies.

"[We are] troubled on every side, yet not distressed; [we are] perplexed, but not in despair;

Persecuted, but not forsaken; cast down, but not destroyed; Always bearing about in the body the dying of the Lord Jesus, that the life also of Jesus might be made manifest in our body. For we which live are always delivered unto death for Jesus' sake, that the life also of Jesus might be made manifest in our mortal flesh. So then death worketh in us, but life in you." 2 Corinthians 4: 8-12

That's because Jesus has given us back more than what Adam lost in the Garden of Eden. The feeling of suicide might pass through our bodies, but we must be strong and prevail. ("And behold I send the promise of my Father upon you: but Tarry ye in the city of Jerusalem, until ye be endued with power from on high." –Luke 24: 49) Consequently, death is at work in us, but life is also. *"But ye are not in the flesh, but in the Spirit, if so be that the Spirit of God dwell in you. Now if any man have not the Spirit of Christ, He is none of His. And if Christ [be] in you, the body [is] dead because of sin; but the Spirit [is] life because of righteousness. But if the Spirit of Him that raised up Jesus from the dead dwell in you, He that raised up Christ from the dead shall also quicken your mortal bodies by His Spirit that dwelleth in you."* Romans 8: 9-11

We must forgive and spread the love and the Word of God. When our hearts are free and pure it's easy to love. When our heads are clear we have good judgment before we can make better decisions. Only if we can fully let our past go and leave the baggage at Calvary we can progress forward. We must stop pointing fingers as if we are without blame. Remember, we are all human and have fallen short at a point. It's hard to watch our people destroy each other over inequity when we all have so much in common. We can't be at war with ourselves and be at war with the enemy, which is the system. When we realize we are all GOD'S CHILDREN, the better off we would be. Most of us are confused in our minds because we allow others to think, speak and influence our life decisions. We must make our own decisions from this point.

Standing on the corner only wastes valuable life time. Running from pain only makes the pain run deeper. Wanting to escape the ghetto is more about escaping the ghetto mindset. We must understand as ghetto people we are all we have and if we destroy each other and our communities then we have nothing. We must better ourselves so we can better our lives and bring our communities closer together. The world hates our love, unity, intelligence, wisdom, power, and we don't even use it. So how do they hate what we don't show or use? Because they know more about our past than we do! It's not our color they hate! We must open our brains and hearts to life and use our God given gifts, talents, dreams, goals, ideas, rights and love for the betterment of mankind.

Disrespecting our parents only brings misery to a disobedient child. We must learn to overlook the garbage and focus on the treasures. Trying to copycat another person will never make us who we are meant to be. What hurts is to know what our ancestors endured to carry us this far and for us to give up and leave our children future-less and hopeless. Now that we have made a little progress we think we have arrived. We turn on each other as if we have made it somewhere. We are still living the same way from the plantation days. We are still living the message Martin Luther King Jr., warned us about.

The only thing change is the technology and the advancement that their invisible empire continues to make. The ghetto is still living in poverty, suffering day in and day out. People who are not from the ghetto are coming into our communities and establishing businesses and taking our legitimate cash. Something we are supposed to be doing. How do these people come to our communities and establish themselves? If these people take their businesses elsewhere then our communities have nothing but clubs.

There are really no black businesses in our communities other than clubs, barber and beauty shops. Since we are so focused on unnecessary tidbits, we don't notice important things but the latest fashion, music and who got what. We think we go through difficult obstacles, but our ancestors went through the hardest tribulations; man put them through hell.

The only thing we go through is selfishness and ignorance to the truth. Our path is clear but we block our own way. Once we move out our own way and allow God to lead we can go on to lead an authentic life and have worldly success. We need to be the men and women we truly are. Understand, I have no problem with you being "that bitch" or "that nigga." Just know the qualities it takes to be a real man or woman. Understand I have no problem with females being on welfare, but the problems come when females take their welfare to take care of a nigga and his friends when her children are starving.

Money brings happiness to those who can buy friends and love. Money keeps us on top of our finance problems, but not our life problems. Money is actually the enemy when we serve it. If money can buy happiness then we can buy our way to Heaven. Money makes us look happy on the outside. Wholeness and self-love brings happiness. Bringing our souls and spirits to life brings happiness. When money doesn't make you happy? What does?

Once we understand the difference between man's government and God's Kingdom we can live a more productive life. Man's government is all about a dollar, power and taking man's God given rights. Of course money can buy our way through America and anything in the world, but what about life after death when money is no longer valuable? Just remember, we all are on a journey back to the source, so just be on your best behavior, because we never know when our time will arrive. What if hell and Heaven is real? Where will you spend everlasting life?

If you thought about the question and don't like the answer you came to, you should seek Jesus. You can always ask Jesus to forgive and accept you; you can also ask him to guide you from where you are in your life now. *"And you, being dead in your sins and the uncircumcision of your flesh, hath he quickened together with him, having forgiven you all trespasses; Blotting out the handwriting of ordinances that was against us, which was contrary to us, and took it out of the way, nailing it to his cross; [And] having spoiled principalities and powers, he made a shew of them openly, triumphing over them in it. Let no man therefore judge you in meat, or in drink, or in respect of an holyday, or of the new moon, or of the sabbath [days]: Which are a shadow of things to come; but the body [is] of Christ."* Colossians 2: 13-17

Chapter 14 – ATTITUDE

"The Negro is indolent and lazy, and spends his money on frivolities, whereas the European is forward-looking, organized and intelligent." - Che Guevara

We all want a better life and the journey we take is the life we achieve. Authenticity leads to worldly success or failure. Either way, life is in the palm of our hands. Adopt a better attitude toward life. Our attitude toward life plays a major part of our paths. Accept God's love and protection. He only wishes us nothing but the best: love, peace, prosperity and everlasting life. When we open our minds and hearts to God and Jesus we reflect them in our attitudes and actions.

"We are living in a time of unbearable dissonance between promise and performance; between good politics and good policy; between professed and practiced family values; between racial creed and racial deed; between calls for community and rampant individualism and greed; and between our capacity to prevent and alleviate human deprivation and disease and our political and spiritual will to do so." -Marian Wright Edelman

We should be tired of wanting to be everything other than men and women and being treated like animals. We should be tired of blaming other folks for our personal decisions. We should be tired of us wanting what Tom has just because we envy him. It's time we help ourselves and grow from selfishness, jealousy, stupidity and greed. One day we are going to realize violence and selfishness is not going to solve our problems.

We need to learn it's not just about us, and learn to give a helping hand and we'd become better people slowly. We all deserve the life Jesus paid for. The only worthy life we are going to get is the one we build and create for ourselves. Ghetto America will never have anything until we get off that foolishness and realize we're a brotherhood &sisterhood that needs to share and evolve with each other. Don't become jealous; become honest, encouraged and inspired to do better for yourself. Money sets us free from debt, but doesn't set our souls free from death; accepting and living in Christ does that. We are to create our future with the present, but we act fearful of the future and expect someone to do it for us. We have been passed the torch, but we're watching the fire die out.

Life is growing stronger by the day, but we're growing weaker because we are carrying this younger mentality through life and expecting to live a fully grown life. We are supposed to be make the future better than the past but we're making it worse. We don't know how good we can have it, we can't because we're too busy worrying about our losses. Our lives are made in these short hours between birth and death.

Look around your communities and see the lives and families affected by our ignorance. If we can affect people's lives negatively then we can positively. We need to take our fate in our hearts and live life. We are too young to waste our valuable life. We have no time to waste. At the end it's the heart that really matters. There are too many opportunities in life than not to take any. We have too much to lose than to keep our heads down and our hearts fearful. Love and passion brings happiness.

Money can't bail us out of life's problems or from death and mom and dad can't always be super (wo)man. We have so much to offer life than to just sit back and watch the days go by without applying any effort.

We have to quit trying to build our lives with no foundation. We are the backbone to our children's lives and the constant growth of America. The ones in control know we exist, but we act as if we don't by feeling sorry for the life we live. We don't pay attention to life. We pay too much attention to the concept of impossible. We limit ourselves, we value the opinions of others too much and that shapes our fears. We have to save ourselves from ourselves. The only thing our hearts are missing is the love of God, once we get His approval we can conquer before the pursuit starts.

"But Jesus beheld [them], and said unto them, With men this is impossible; but with God all things are possible." -Matthew 19: 26

The last thing the politicians want is for the truth to be released to us. Some of us got this image stuck in our minds that if we get caught with a book that we're looking stupid or like a geek. Books will get us more progress and power than a gun or ignorance will. You think they want us to have anything other than an 8x10 room with just walls and separated from life and family. Every evil deed returns to its owner.

Chapter 15- THOSE POINTS

"One of the things that has to be faced is the process of waiting to change the system, how much we have got to do to find out who we are, where we have come from and where we are going."
-Ella Baker

We all come to those points in our lives, when we don't know where to go from the last steps of the past. We ask ourselves where I go from here. I say, go in the direction you want to see your life like, take those step into the unknown, walk by faith and not by sight. Your sense of destiny will help you in your pursuit for success. Go for whatever it is you think you deserve but don't have yet. There will be a time for change. We have to learn to make peace with the past. We must exchange our weaknesses for strength, poverty for prosperity, our emptiness for wholeness and hate for love. We must challenge our dark past for an unknown bright future. It costs so much to live, but it's free because Jesus paid the price in full, He owes no debt. ***"Stand fast therefore in the liberty wherewith Christ hath made us free, and be not entangled again with the yoke of bondage."*** -Galatians 5: 1

The way is clear and free, we just have to learn to put mind over matter. We block the way with doubt and fear and no understanding of who we are or our lives' purposes. Bring the fire back to life. If we don't fix our problems now then the future of our children will be like the 3rd world children we see on television with no parents, food and no place to stay; but in a hut. Our actions and behavior is leading them to that life. We need to realize it before it's too late.

We are to make a life out of nothing. Life has more of a meaning than just talents, dreams, money and materials; it has a calling, a purpose. To fulfill our divine purpose, we have to answer when we're called. We can't be afraid to face the world against all the odds. Just know in our hearts we are free, but in our minds we feel trapped because of different reasons. The power that makes our desires, dreams and visions a reality is not our environment or any condition outside ourselves; it's within the heart, minds and spirit it's the way we think and believe. I believe that is what it means to walk by faith and not sight.

Faith is the evidence of something hoped for and prayed for, and our sight sometimes gives us a vision of hopelessness. One of the greatest weaknesses of a human is doubt and self-pity. Our bodies shouldn't be our only worries, such as: shoes, clothes, houses, and cars. What truly matters is the inner person, our minds, hearts, our decisions and life after death. Man has great abilities we barely know we have.

"There's a lot of Americans, black and white, who think that we've arrived where we need to be and nothing else needs to be done and affirmative action needs to be dismantled." -Spike Lee

SCHOOL

Education is a huge part of life and makes a substantial difference. Due to our mindless behavior problems, violence and peer pressure and everything else that goes on we rarely pay attention to school. People think school is not really needed but it is. Students normally take their personal problems into school, not really focusing. We need to learn to separate our problems and deal with them one at a time. Some students now-a-days only go to school to show off their new things and when the new things are old things they rarely show up. Thinking school is a fashion show, we need to teach our children school is no fashion show or playground.

Education doesn't care what kind of shoes or clothes we wear.

School only cares about what we learn; we need to teach our children school is here to help them along the way. Why must our children not even try or put forth an effort? They seem to take school for a joke and think they don't need an education. Why must our school seem more like a prison; why won't we pay attention to the bigger picture and choose to be ignorant?

I know people who only apply for college just for the financial aid and when the check came they dropped out. The school would receive their payment and they would give the balance to the student. Several days after receiving the payment, you no longer see the student. Had they stayed in school, there's no telling where life and the education would have taken them, or what they could have accomplished. If only people get money off their minds all the time we can allow our lives to be free. Everybody wants money but many are not paying attention to the four words that made this country great: IN GOD WE TRUST!

Get your education. Who cares if you look like a geek because you want to learn? Laugh at those people who make fun of you. Don't feel sorry for yourself if you can't go to school in the up to date trends. Your time will come when you will shine; just educate yourself in and out of school. They used to burn our schools and churches, but now, in the 21 century, we don't want to walk in neither one of them. America wasn't built for us; it was built by us, around us and against us. That's why it is important we learn and teach our children to learn about God. That's the foundation of life: education and God. We have to apply ourselves. Push yourself into new realms and ask questions when you don't understand something. This is the only way you will learn, develop, and grow mentally and emotionally. Don't assume learning stops when you leave school.

Two Different Americas in one Country

America never expected for us to be free. We live in two different Americas, in the ghetto our laws, language and life is totally different from the American way of life. We have never been a part of the American way of life, even though we help them create such a wonderful life. America is supposed to have life, liberty, the pursuit of happiness, justice and prosperity for all. The Ghetto-American life is totally the opposite, due to the pain, poverty, stress, anxiety, division and the lack of pursuits. There are millions of people, children, babies, young men and women struggling with America and their stolen identity.

Asking themselves if they should go to school, should they sell drugs, or sell themselves; living on a day to day decision with no hope of a future. Parents today don't even notice the needs of their children, such as the silent pains, the mental and emotional guidance they need; letting the children make the decisions the parents should be making. Parents today act as if they fear their children. Why must the Ghetto-American children be faced with so many obstacles at such an early age, from the home life to the school life?

Our children feel hopeless in a hopeful life. We look upon each other with pity instead of faith. Why must our people fight America's wars when America is at war with us? America doesn't acknowledge us, but in a way I can't blame them because we don't even acknowledge us anymore, so they take advantage of that. The American flag doesn't stand for our freedom as Ghetto-Americans because we're still in bondage. We didn't gain our freedom July 4, 1776. The 4th is the birthday of America's National Independence, and the Europeans political freedom from the British. Does the American flag represent the country as a whole, or the European race? We gained our freedom September 22, 1862 and I don't think we truly understand what that date means. It's a day that should be cherished and celebrated. The day we became free there was a power and control struggle; something we don't really understand. The history of our people would never be understood because we barely understand today.

After the Emancipation we flooded their cities in the late 1800 and earlier 1900s and populated out of their control. We are 2nd class citizens in their eyes; to them we are ruining what they work so hard to create. As we can see they don't want to share with us, but the Constitution requires we share the land. As we get ignorant they continue to build their empire. Nothing has changed, but time and the generations, not the message. We represent the past, present and the future. We are the 21st century generation. What are we going to do with our freedom?

People don't want to hear about the pain and suffering of the ghetto, or the children who go to bed hungry at night because the mother is addict and the father is… who's to say? No one wants to discuss young people with no place to sleep at night. Who cares, until it happens to them? People no longer focus on the importance of these issues because we have been brainwashed and now we are brain washing the next generation with lies and giving them a hopeless future from our unconscious minds. We can change our way of life together.

We must somehow find a way to help each other, we must come together. We must become one again, time is being wasted. We need a Godly solution for the ghetto crisis. We're at the point of no returning in our communities. I can't do it by myself and you can't either, but we can together. We must change our attitude toward life and each other and realize our ghettos are our communities and our part of our 40 acres. We can no longer wait on Superman to rescue us from the ghetto, we must rescue the ghetto. Once we change our attitude and mental set we can change our lives and the ghettoes.

We're in the right place, but our minds are in the wrong places. We're standing on a broken promised land because we won't patch the pieces together. I have faith in us all to heal our broken hearts, souls and life, but my faith isn't enough; you need to have it too. Know that God answers to faith. We can't allow our weaknesses of fear to paralyze us from using the power of faith. Faith and prayer are the most powerful things on earth.

We can only be destroyed by believing and becoming what others want us to be. One of our problems is we think like others and not for ourselves. We are part of this environment and the only way the ghetto is going to survive is to stick together. We need to educate ourselves with the information at hand. People without knowledge are like trees without roots. It's important we know our history and to know our history we must go deeper than the American text books. Go to the original source!

We must educate ourselves on life, on GOD'S WORD, on our history and on ourselves. We need to recognize our greatness. We have a life to live so let's step out the shadows. Everything we need and want is within our grasp; we just don't recognize it. If we fail at life, it's not because of nobody else, it's because of what and who we chose to honor or serve. Our future is determined by who or what we chose to honor and look up to. If we can succeed in our minds we can succeed in life.

Our minds need goals and education; our hearts need love, and our spirits need spiritual guidance. If our minds don't have a picture of the future it will always replay the past. We can't allow the enemy to deceive our minds and hearts because it affects our personal lives, pockets and our families' lives. We can't sit around and drown in our own sorrows, while others go on with life. We must prove our strength to ourselves. We have enough scars; we don't need to add more to ourselves.

The government only cares about making profit off of us, and we support everyone else except each other. Abraham Lincoln, John Brown, John F. Kennedy, Martin Luther King Jr. , Malcolm X, Merger Evers and many others were killed because they stood for our freedom and the rights of men. Now we are placing our freedom right back in their hands. I don't understand how we can't appreciate the love and the lives that were given and taken to get us here. We have been in chains and under control since the beginning of America and before America. Even Jesus gave His life, not just for us but for mankind.

We are to secure the existence of our people and secure a future for our children. We are to teach our children their history of where we are from and how we got here to help them grow physically, mentally, emotionally, spiritually, socially, academically and knowledgeable with self-expression.

We are to teach our children who they are and what they stand for and the importance of school and life, and the difference between material beauty and self-beauty. We can raise our children to be a stronger and a better generation. We can't raise our children to be ignored. Our children are one day our future.

"I believe the children are our future. Teach them well and let them lead the way. Show them all the beauty they possess inside. Give them a sense of pride to make it easier." -Whitney Houston

Our children do what they see us do, so we must set a good example. Understand street knowledge only gets us so far, we can use street knowledge and life knowledge to get ahead. We can go beyond the ghetto life and have a fabulous life; only if we remember the lessons it taught us. Understand, the government hates the freedom of speech, so don't fall back, take the stand, don't be afraid to be fearless. Choose your allegiances wisely; being loyal to a gang, the streets, or anything that serves you no good is like being loyal to the devil. You can be loyal to your people and still not be a follower. Be loyal to serving your purpose.

Each day is a given gift, not a right, and we can't take the free ride in our own lives. We all know nothing is free but life. A new day is like God saying 'wake up, I'm not finish with you, now go live and pursue life, go make a difference, go spread My love, go help My children set their souls free.' Only He know what's a day truly holds secrets.

"These things have I spoken unto you, that my joy might remain in you, and [that] your joy might be full. This is my commandment, That ye love one another, as I have loved you. Greater love hath no man than this, that a man lay down his life for his friends. Ye are my friends, if ye do whatsoever I command you. Henceforth I call you not servants; for the servant knoweth not what his lord doeth: but I have called you friends; for all things that I have heard of my Father I have made known unto you." John 15: 11-15

"The inability to get health care because people lack insurance, kills, less traumatically, and less visibly than terrorism, but the result is the same. And poor housing and poor education and low wages kills the spirit and the capacity and the quality of life that all of us deserve." -Marian Wright Edelman

We are now at the point where we chain ourselves and allow others to think and make decisions for us. We turn on each other only to be turned on. They show us no fear but they are fearful of us, so they make us fear ourselves and life. When there is nothing to fear but God, why fear man? We show them too much fear. Fear is a big factor, but we're a powerful part of God. We must understand the only thing we need is to turn on our light. We must understand we are all unique with different ideas, gifts, talents and purposes that must be used to better serve humanity. We are too young to just sit back and watch life pass by and not accomplish anything, but a child and a jail cell.

We've got to look at life beyond the American standards and dream bigger. We've got to cut the negative people out our lives even though we love them; they are a source of the problem. These people are what make us lose focus on the main goals. Somewhere down the line, someone installed one goal in our mind and that one goal became our way of thinking/living.

Nothing gets done in the ghetto because we all pursue the same path. If we have to step away from friends or whatever's holding us back no goal is unattainable. If we as people would make more conscious decisions, then we could live an abundant beautiful life. We are not going to solve our personal or public issues being ignorant to the truth.

I don't think we understand that economics, health, education, social justice, civic engagement, and inequality still exist in America today. It's one thing to know it exists and another to do something about it. Our problems will never be fixed as long as we are focused on the non-important things. We're falling short because of lack of understanding and knowledge of what's going on in life and the lack of visions, purpose and destiny that's not being fulfilled. The thoughts and attitudes of most of us place us in a position to fail, rather than the other way around. If we are going to fulfill our potential and pursue destiny; we've got to get rid of the selfishness and the ignorant mentality.

Learn to forgive and move forward. We've got to show the world that we are more than just ghetto people. Our ancestors proved to the world that we were more than just slaves, so why not carry on with the same strength and faith, but stronger? With our support we can and we will be forever free and conquer hate and poverty. We got to learn to get along with different people from different back grounds.

The best ability in life is to love and to know we can achieve greatness and to help others know they can too. We have to take steps inside and outside the ghetto to shine our light. We, as Ghetto-Americans, have unlimited power and influence that we use the wrong way. In a way, I don't blame America, because we allow them to make fools of us. We can't be negative about nothing, not our past, families, friends, or finances. Develop a positive attitude, it will help you live a positive and powerful life, just be grateful for who you are and what you have.

Why must there be one America but on one side there is total despair and poverty and on the other side, America the flattering promise? What have the African race done to be treated like 3/5ths of a human? Why must we give them all power, why must we hear their voice but they won't listen to ours? We American people have within our power to free ourselves and subdue the government, without violence. Just look at the failure of the reconstruction to see all the former slaves who made it to the capitol from a plantation. After the Emancipation we had blacks in the U. S offices until the early 1900s when Woodrow Wilson took office and fired them all and restored white supremacy. It's not that America can't become one, it's just we give too much power to one race in America and American politics don't want to accept us.

"The life of the nation is secure only while the nation is honest, truthful and virtuous." -Frederick Douglass.

Chapter 16 – CONCLUSION

"We are moving from one state of organization to another, and we shall continue until we have thoroughly lifted ourselves in the organization of GOVERNMENT." -Marcus Garvey

America is a gift from God to the world, but the politicians have made it a competition for dominance. We have been misguided for too long now. It's too many races in America to only notice one race of people. If the United States government is not going to work with us to help build our communities and people, then we must do it ourselves. We have to establish and govern ourselves and stand in defense of anyone trying to conquer us. We are an anarchy and confused race of what's going on outside our ghettoes. We have lost our way on life's path and we need to turn this conspiracy life around mentally, spiritually, physically and financially. We can't say we don't care because we elected Obama. The whole goal for us coming to America was to build an empire without us knowing we were building one. If we can help build their empire we can build our own. They're not trying to agree with us or come up with no solution to help us out of the situation they put us in; we have to do it ourselves.

Take a moment to realize all that we have been through over the years and centuries, to come to this point. Everything that happened from the days of Toussaint L'ouverture, slavery, until the day of Rosa Parks, Martin L. King Jr. , Malcolm X, Merger Ever and Brown v. The Board of Education in the 1950s-60s, still affects us to this day. They gave us a little bit of something to confuse our minds, but the problem is much bigger than our material wants.

They don't need to destroy us now; we do it for them and don't even care. The only thing that needs to be destroyed is racism, greed, ignorance, hate and selfishness. If we're not killing and selling drugs or breaking in each other's' houses, they rarely have a case to convict us. Based on what I see in communities after communities and reported on the daily news, these are the main reasons, our people are locked up.

We must realize it's the entire ghetto in struggle and pain; when we realize we need each other then we can build a better future for ourselves, our children and their children. They don't hate us because we're ghetto and poor people. They hate our will to survive, our courage and strength to fight and challenge their system, our determination, our drive and our love for God and one another. The possibility we can rule this country, if we're willing to learn and take risks. They want to conquer any race or land of people, who is willing to settle for defeat only to keep the European race in power, wealth and land. They hate us because we embody life, liberty and the pursuit of happiness. We can't enter our adult life with minimal education about our lives, ourselves, history or the world as a whole. We can't become victim to our minds or our lives.

A black man being in the White House is not going to fix 400 years of problems in four years, or eight years. The problems in the White House are the European-Americans' problems. Do you think they have time to worry about our issues? Do you think they wake up in the morning with "niggers' problems" on their minds? They are too busy worrying about other countries' problems and don't want to fix their own country's problems. If we can fill the jails, grave yards, sports centers, studios, clubs, and streets, then we should be able to fill the White House.

There's nothing wrong with being an athlete or rapper, just know we are so much more than just that. Even though we have those talents, that doesn't mean that's all we're meant to do or be. We have it within our grasp to make changes. It's up to us to solve our own cultural problems. We need more of our people in the White House; we need more people in the democratic and republican, parties and in the congress to represent us. If we get just a few more of our people in office then we have some say so on how this country is ran.

We need to quit falling victim to the system and learn it. We need to quit complaining about what they aren't giving us and work twice as hard for what we want and need. We need just as much power, wealth and land as they do. We need more faith believers in the office; it doesn't matter the race, as long as they are willing to stand for what's right by God. It's time we not just focus on the European race and history, but on our own race and history.

America is not just an European country, it's The United States of America; and in America there are many races of people, but only one human race. We must increase our education and our value of life. We MUST, MUST, MUST, TAKE THE LIMITS OFF GOD!!! We need not be afraid of God in the wrong way, but have respect and love for God. Know that He is all powerful and will do what His Word says. God loves us and this world. We don't have to hide from God because of our sins. He forgave us; so we don't need to run from Him, run to Him. God does not expect us to be perfect, He expects us to press on with faith in Him.

Have faith in God, life and in yourself. Know the only person we have to answer to is God, based on the life we live here on Earth. Enjoy life, enjoy your family, enjoy your home; there is so much GOD wants to do in your life and through your life. We are warrior children of GOD and the only battle we have is faith vs. fear. We have the power to free ourselves with our voices, love, faith, power and with the pursuit. The words we speak contain power, so if we speak doubt, poor words, or if we speak faith and prosperity, that's what our lives become. *"A man's belly shall be satisfied with the fruit of his mouth; [and] with the increase of his lips shall he be filled. Death and life [are] in the power of the tongue: and they that love it shall eat the fruit thereof."* Proverbs 18: 20-21

We have so much to fix and there's so much to be done in our personal lives and in our communities. In order for us to know where we are in our lives we have to go back to history; before the assassinations, drugs, crimes and division hit our communities. Most of our communities don't have jobs, playgrounds, stores, decent homes, or sports fields. The only things our communities have are despair and poverty. Folks just stand around feeling sorry for themselves; well, no more of that. Our communities are not impoverished, our minds are. We can change our impoverish communities by upgrading our minds and education by making smarter decisions.

Bad and challenging things are going to come our way but we can and will overcoming them with faith and dedication to the task at hand, and by sticking together. As I used this scripture above, I chose to end my book by using it again as I feel it is very powerful. ("These things that I've spoken unto you that in Me you will have peace. In the world you will have tribulation, but be of good cheer, I have overcome the world." -John 16: 33)

The Europeans chose to bring us to America for their purpose so if they had a purpose to bring us here God has a higher purpose for us staying here. *"But ye [are] a chosen generation, a royal priesthood, an holy nation, a peculiar people; that ye should shew forth the praises of him who hath called you out of darkness into his marvellous light: Which in time past [were] not a people, but [are] now the people of God: which had not obtained mercy, but now have obtained mercy."* 1 Peter 2-9: 10

I want you to know there is so much more to life than just being a criminal, baby mama, baby daddy or what the world calls nobodies. We have an identity, not just an image. A ghetto person with faith, love, power, intelligence, riches and wits is an insult to the Europeans because they expect us to have a mind of a wild animal. We, as a race, struggle against powerful forces that prey on our ignorance and our weaknesses to stand and provide for ourselves.

The sad thing about it is that poverty and ignorance is not just in one ghetto community, it's in all ghetto communities across America.

We have to resolve to no longer teach our children how to fall victim. We must grow into fully grown adults and show our children that life is worth living. Don't run from pain, embrace it; it helps us grow. Our journey has only just started, so go on with the tears of pain and joy. As long as we live, we are who we are and nothing will ever change it, so love yourself.

I have no problem with a person being on welfare or staying in the projects, just know you are not trapped; you have the will power and desires inside you to prevail. If we believe, dream and give God thanks then we can achieve with time and effort. If we are smart enough to survive with the little resources we have now, what do you think would happen if you added education, to your street survival mentality? Maybe you would become a successful entrepreneur.

Drug dealers, nobody is mad at you for wanting to make riches. Drugs are a target for our people and our communities and laws made against us, so when they do their drug busts they take your life and the lives of our families and spend all the drug money. What do you think they do with the drug money besides continue to build their empire and use it as contraband?

Drug dealers, I wish you were smart and strong enough to get out the drug game and invest your money into something more productive. Nothing will change until we change ourselves and our thinking. Our heartache can and will be abolished, if we pursue to overcome it. We can't hate ourselves because of the situations we were born into. We shouldn't bring children into our lives if we are not stable enough to care for them. We must provide shelter, food, clothes, and the necessities, they are going to need: love, guidance and protection, not just gear.

Anybody can have sex and produce a child, but it takes a fully mature person to accept their responsibilities. Do you really want your children going through the same heartrending life you lived? There's a way through life that is hopeful, our ghetto mentality is hopeless. If you want to leave the ghetto have a plan and know why you want to leave and know what you're going to do when you leave. Ask yourself do you really want to live this ghetto way of life for the rest of your life. If so or if not, examine your lifestyle and friends and see where you're headed and what you can do to better your life, instead of making life more difficult.

We need to rehabilitate our lives, mend our broken hearts, and restore our families and communities. We have to come together; we need the united strength, power, faith, respect and love from one another. Once we stand back in the protection and love of God we will conquer forever. One way or another, we have to extinguish our fears and face reality. We just have to remove the excuses we make up. We have everything within us we need to live a beautifully abundant life. Persevere to help restore a broken world/system.

The American government is so untrustworthy, but America is an awesome country. However, the corruption and greed is ruining it. (*"The king of judgment establisheth land: but he that receiveth gifts overthroweth it."* -Proverbs 29:4.) We gotta get back on track with daily life and GOD, and also face reality, no matter how much it hurts. Is your life worth the pursuit of happiness or are you just going to give up and fall victim? We must realize as ghetto people we are all we have, and our communities are all we got in the U. S. A. If we keep destroying either one it's only us we're destroying. The hole we were born into is not deep. It only seems deep because of the shadows that stands over us, it deepens as we sit still in our sorrow. America is a great country and the folks outside America notice it, but the folks on the inside take it for granted.

America is a one of a kind country; it's the last hope of the world's freedom! I know it seems like poverty, pain, suffering and oppression will never end. It will; we just can't continue to give in to it. We'll get through because love won't let us fail. There's a place inside us where our faith and love begin; we should reach for it and use it. It's important that we know that it's not just life and its difficulties that we have to conquer, but it's the self within that's the greatest battles of them all.

Talents, goals, dreams, ideas, and faith are dead until sown in the garden of life, with the nutrition that's needed to harvest and developed a wonderful and abundant life. God asks us to give and it will be given. He asks for a tenth, but we place everything before Him like bills, furniture, cars materials, entertainment, but we always want something from Him and wonder why He isn't doing this or that when we want Him to do it. *"But seek ye first the kingdom of God and all these things shall be added unto you."* Matthew 6: 33

I believe we can and will break the generational curse that plagues our lives. I know we can make a greater comeback if we stop with the hate, jealously and the useless violence.

"Praise ye the LORD. Blessed [is] the man [that] feareth the LORD, [that] delighteth greatly in his commandments. His seed shall be mighty upon earth: the generation of the upright shall be blessed." Psalms 112: 1-2

If you need help don't be afraid to ask, even if you hear no, don't stop the pursuit to happiness. We know the truth, now it's time to acknowledge it. Once we get our minds together, release the stress and cure our insanity. We're a new generation of people, let's cast the old mentality out; we need to not be each other's enemies anymore. We're a new breed; we're not Africans or Americans, we are African-Americans, the best of both worlds.

In America, all a ghetto person has is each other, without each other what do we have? We are one of the best generations ever, and let's not give up because of the heart pain and mind stress, we came too far. We are destined to rise; we have been rising since the days of slavery to the day of Obama. Let's keep on. We hold the pieces to complete the puzzle. We're the answers that can solve the mysteries. We're the key that can unlock our understanding; it's all inside of us. We have everything we need to overcome, so let's keep Martin Luther King Jr. and our dream alive; we can't let it die.

Along the pursuit we will come across our kudos, so be bold. If we don't define ourselves the people of the world will. All we have to do is have faith, keep our minds clear, humble hearted and grounded with our heads held up and we will weather whatever storms come our way. The ambitions that lives within you will help you progress when times gets rough, encourage yourself. Persevere and make sure you are relentless in your pursuit of your goals.

As we pursue life we shouldn't become content with our lives or the world we live in because there always more to be done. Always live with a contented soul rested in Christ to have a relationship with God. Martin Luther King said in his last speech: "I just want to do God's Will. And He's allowed me to go up to the mountain. And I've looked over. And I've seen the Promised Land. I may not get there with you. But I want you to know tonight, that we, as a people, will get to the Promised Land. My eyes have seen the coming of the Lord!"

"When the righteous are in authority, the people rejoice: but when the wicked beareth rule, the people mourn." Proverbs 29: 2

From the life of slavery look at how far we have come and look at what it took to get us here. We wouldn't be here if our ancestors wouldn't paved the way to freedom with only faith and praising God. It is only by faith that we will move to higher ground, we need to have faith in Him who has never failed and will never leave nor forsake us! The march to freedom is still a distance away, but we have come too far to just give up now.

The American dream is for any person of any race to have life, liberty and the pursuit of happiness. The pursuit of happiness is to strive to fix what we don't like about our lives and to correct the oppression of the government. The moment we face our fears is the day our lives change forever. It's up to us to accept the challenge it won't be easy, but the journey has started.

We must realize our personal powers and our culture's power. I pray someday we will come to understand GOD'S Word and His power, and reunite ourselves with our culture and live to serve His purpose. We don't have to be a copycat to fit in. If you don't fit in, that means you were meant to stand out. We can't play the victim role because then we become the victim. We will never live up to our full potential if we become the victim.

"The love the strength the history the passion, The courage of an impoverished people, That the world once abandoned Shining infinite everlasting now!" –Lupe Fiasco

Much love and many blessings! GOD BLESS!

"Blessed [is] every one that feareth the LORD; that walketh in his ways. For thou shalt eat the labour of thine hands: happy [shalt] thou [be], and [it shall be] well with thee." Psalms 128: 1-2

Sincerely, Julius L. Edwards

www.ingramcontent.com/pod-product-compliance
Lightning Source LLC
Chambersburg PA
CBHW022304060426
42446CB00007BA/581